ATTENTION:
BAR CODE IS L
INSIDE OF BOOK
P9-BIL-943

PELÉ:
A Biography

OTHER BOOKS BY JIM/JAMES HASKINS

DIARY OF A HARLEM SCHOOLTEACHER
RESISTANCE: PROFILES IN NONVIOLENCE
REVOLUTIONARIES: AGENTS OF CHANGE
THE WAR AND THE PROTEST: VIETNAM
PROFILES IN BLACK POWER
A PIECE OF THE POWER: FOUR BLACK MAYORS
FROM LEW ALCINDOR TO KAREEM ABDUL-JABBAR
BLACK MANIFESTO FOR EDUCATION (EDITOR)
RELIGIONS
THE PSYCHOLOGY OF BLACK LANGUAGE
with Hugh F. Butts, M.D.
JOKES FROM BLACK FOLKS
PINCKNEY BENTON STEWART PINCHBACK
RALPH BUNCHE: A MOST RELUCTANT HERO
ADAM CLAYTON POWELL: PORTRAIT OF A MARCHING BLACK
WITCHCRAFT, MYSTICISM AND MAGIC IN THE BLACK WORLD
STREET GANGS: YESTERDAY AND TODAY
BABE RUTH AND HANK AARON: THE HOME RUN KINGS
SNOW SCULPTURE AND ICE CARVING: THE ART OF CREATING TRANSIENT FORMS
THE CONSUMER MOVEMENT
THE PICTURE LIFE OF MALCOLM X
FIGHTING SHIRLEY CHISHOLM
THE CREOLES OF COLOR OF NEW ORLEANS
DOCTOR J: A BIOGRAPHY OF JULIUS ERVING
YOUR RIGHTS: PAST AND PRESENT
THE STORY OF STEVIE WONDER

PELÉ: A Biography

James S. Haskins

DOUBLEDAY & COMPANY, INC.
GARDEN CITY, NEW YORK 1976

Acknowledgments

I am grateful to Julia Auerbacher for her help, to Maurice Coelho for translating much of the source material, to Mary Ellen Arrington, who typed the manuscript, and to Kathy Benson, without whom this book would not have been possible.

ISBN 0-385-11565-2
Library of Congress Catalog Card Number 75-39123

Printed in the United States of America
First Edition

Contents

Part One
The Game of Soccer

1 Soccer Around the World

In the United States, when you hear the word *football,* you immediately think of the New York Jets and the Miami Dolphins, of O. J. Simpson, of touchdowns and field goals. But in every other country except the United States and Canada, the word *football* means an entirely different game and calls to mind very different images. It is called *futeball* in some languages and *futbol* in others, but it seems that everywhere there's a name for it. It is also more popular in every other country in the world than "our" football. It is the game people in North America call soccer.

At any rate, based on what is actually done with the ball, soccer should be called football in the United States, and Canada, too, for it is a game that involves constant contact between the feet and the ball. While occasionally the head can be used, use of the hands at any time during a soccer game, except by the goalkeeper, is absolutely illegal. By contrast, in North American-style football, the feet come into contact with the ball only a relatively few times during the game compared to the number of times it is thrown and caught and carried with the hands.

It is not, however, the intention here to start a campaign in favor of calling soccer football in the United States and leaving the Jets and Dolphins to come up with a new name for the game they play. Rather, it is the aim here to introduce the reader to the most popular game in the world, and to perhaps the most popular player in the history of the game, Pelé (pronounced Peh-lay). Pelé is now in the United States playing for the New York soccer team, the Cosmos. He is here for one major reason, and that is to bring soccer to the same level of popularity as the other spectator sports in the United States. Within the past decade or so, soccer has been increasing in popularity on the grass-roots level in the United States, and Pelé might excite massive national interest. Heaven knows soccer needs all the help along those lines that it can get. After all, it's been around in this country for well over two hundred years.

It has been suggested that soccer failed to "catch

on" in this country during most of those years because it is not rough-and-tumble enough. U.S. sports fans like charging, hard-hitting, knock-down action, and they like their games full of scores and interruptions. This is why U.S.-style football, basketball, and hockey are so popular. By contrast, soccer is, at its best anyway, closer to ballet—fluid, graceful, and intricate. And often, the goals themselves are not as important as how they are made.

Basically, soccer is a very simple game, as the considerable number of how-to books available show. It is played on a good-sized field, but actual dimensions are quite flexible. A soccer field can be anywhere from 100 to 130 yards long and from 50 to 100 yards wide, but generally a field measuring 115 yards long and 75 yards wide is preferred. As in football or basketball, the field length is divided exactly in half by a line, and each team claims one half as its own. Like basketball courts, in the center of the line is a circle. Usually having a radius of 10 yards, it is where play begins at the start of the game, at the beginning of the second half, and after each goal.

At each end of the field stands a goal. A frame 8 yards wide and 8 feet high supports netting that slopes diagonally to the ground outside the playing field. Inside the playing field, surrounding the goal and its net, is a space 44 yards by 18 yards. It is the penalty area.

A soccer team has 11 members. Ten of them wear uniforms of the same color. These are the forwards, halfbacks (midfielders, linkmen), and fullbacks (defenders). The goalkeeper wears a different color, to avoid confusion, for he alone can touch the ball with his hands. The ball is multicolored, often black and white and smaller than a basketball, being 27 to 28 inches in diameter. The game length is 90 minutes, divided into two 45-minute halves. There are no time-outs except in the case of serious injury or to put the ball back into play. Therefore, anyone who plays soccer must be in excellent shape. In an average professional game, a player runs between 7 and 10 miles, including nearly a mile at top speed!

To start the game, a coin is tossed, and the team that wins the toss may either kick off or receive, in which case it chooses the goal it wants to defend. When the kickoff occurs, the opposing team must be at least ten yards into its own half of the field. The kickoff is not like that of American football. It is a short kick by the center forward to one of his teammates. As soon as the kickoff has been made, the ball is in play, and it remains in play until it goes over the goal line, out of bounds across one of the sidelines, or into the goal net. All the players except the two goalies are constantly changing their positions, the team on offense trying to get the ball into their opponents' net and the team on defense trying to get it away and into the other team's net.

There are eight basic techniques employed by the ten members of each team who move up and down the field. Five are ball-handling techniques used by the players in control of the ball.

Kicking, in which height and length are not as important as speed and accuracy, can be done in several ways and using different parts of the foot.

Passing can also be done in different ways and with different parts of the foot. It is the basis for successful team play, and the best teams are those that employ clever passing from one member to another to get the ball downfield.

Dribbling is not at all like dribbling in basketball. In soccer, it means controlling and moving the ball with the feet while running down the field.

Heading is the most highly developed technique that involves a part of the body other than the feet. Other parts of the body except for the hands and arms may be used, but there is not much control in the chest. The head, specifically the center of the forehead, can be used as effectively as the feet.

Trapping is getting control of the ball when it is

coming toward the player in the air or on the ground. This can be done by using the head, body, legs, or feet to stop the ball's progress so that its direction can be controlled.

Of course, while the team with the ball is kicking and passing and dribbling and heading and trapping, the opposing team members are trying to get the ball away. They may not strike their opponents, or kick them, jump at them, or trip them. And of course they may not touch the ball with their hands. The three major techniques they use are obstructing, tackling, and charging.

Obstructing, also called blocking, is a method of slowing the forward progress of an opponent by moving slowly in front of him and forcing him to change direction.

Tackling in soccer is not at all like the technique in football. In soccer, it means to get the ball away from an opponent through clever use of the feet, and without tripping the opponent.

Charging is a method used to unbalance an opponent, and is the most violent defensive technique. A player can charge right into an opponent who has the ball and knock him off-balance, but he may use only his shoulder in making contact, and one foot must be kept on the ground.

Meanwhile, the goalies watch tensely, for it is

largely up to them to defend the goal and keep the ball from going into the net. They may use any part of the body to do so, including leaping into the air and catching the ball with both hands, throwing themselves on top of the ball, or throwing their bodies lengthwise on the ground in front of the net to stop a ground ball. The tensest time for a goalkeeper is when some defensive foul has been called in the penalty area in front of the goal and the referee awards a penalty kick to the offensive team. Then only the goalkeeper is between the kicker and the huge net, and none of his teammates can help him.

When the ball gets past the goalkeeper and into the net, whether on a regular kick or pass or on a penalty kick, it counts one point. Scoring goals is very difficult, as it is in hockey, and soccer game scores are never very high: 2–1, 3–1, 1–0, etc. The excitement of soccer is obviously not in high scores, nor is it in rough-and-tumble play (which hockey, also a low-scoring game, has). The excitement of soccer is in its intricate footwork, its tremendous body control, its fast pace, and its beautifully choreographed teamwork. Compared to the skills of other major team sports, those of soccer are hard to measure. Baseball has its statistics, like RBIs, triples, doubles, etc.; basketball has its statistics, like assists.

Ty Cobb, Babe Ruth, and Hank Aaron can be compared statistically almost down to the number of times they took off their caps to wipe their brows. Other than numbers of goals scored, there are few statistics in the annals of soccer on the basis of which to compare Pelé with, say, Stanley Matthews, the English star who played from the 1930s to the 1950s, or the Portuguese star, Eusebio, who became famous in the 1960s and who, incidentally, was signed by the Boston Minutemen shortly after Pelé signed with the Cosmos.

The term *world* is used pretty casually in titling athletic competitions. In baseball, the World Series includes teams from no other part of the world but the United States. Even the Little League World Series excluded Taiwan, after Taiwan teams won too many of the championships. But soccer's World Cup series have included teams from Uruguay and Czechoslovakia, Sweden and Spain, Brazil and the United States, Germany and the Soviet Union, and many other countries. And long before the World Cup competition was begun in 1930, soccer was played in various forms in all of those countries and more. It is the most international sport in the world.

Like all games, soccer began very simply. Kicking a round object about is a perfectly natural thing for a young person to do—at least today. In earlier centuries, it was a perfectly natural thing for a young *boy* to do. Young boys grew to be men, and if they had enjoyed the competition of their childhood game, they continued to play it. Evidence from thousands of years ago of the playing of some sort of game involving kicking a round ball about can be found in the histories of China, Japan, Britain, and Italy. And who knows how many other areas had such games but did not or could not record their existence?

In China, the game was played as far back as 206 B.C., under the name of *Tsu Chu,* which roughly translated means "Must kick the stuffed leather ball." A special match was played every year near the royal pavilion in honor of the Emperor's birthday, and the Emperor, Ch'eng Ti, was himself an accomplished player. The goals were made of two bamboo posts thirty feet high with a silk net a yard wide attached to them. Winners of the special matches were rewarded richly; the losers, depending on the Emperor's mood, were either flogged or beheaded!

A Japanese version of the game, called *Kemari,* was played over fourteen hundred years ago. It was very ceremonial, and much less emotionally charged than the Chinese game. The Greeks played a game called *harpaston,* in which a sand-filled ball was used. It was similar to the *harpastium* played in Rome, and which the Roman conquerors of the ancient Britons are said to have introduced to the conquered areas.

The Bretons and Normans in northern France had a game called *soule,* which they probably introduced to Britain in 1066 when William the Conqueror invaded that country. There were no actual fields or even boundaries in *soule,* and in fact distance was of major importance. A team could run for miles, passing a leather or wooden ball back and forth among them, before their opponents managed to catch up with them and get the ball away!

England is credited as the birthplace of soccer as we know it today because it was the first country in which an actual association governing the sport was formed. The English kept records of the game beginning about the middle of the fourteenth century, when the English royalty, who had long looked down on this "football" privately, began to do so publicly and officially.

Soccer was a game of the lower classes, and it was a rough, often dangerous sport. Matches, particularly between rival towns, frequently resulted in serious injuries and even deaths. From 1349 onward, various British monarchs either spoke out against it or actually prohibited it.

There were exceptions, notably William, prince of Orange, later William III of England. Before his arrival in England, William's interest had been sparked by Count Albemarle, who returned from Italy in 1681 with reports of a game called *calcio* that he had seen in Florence. *Calcio* differed from the type of soccer known in England because it allowed the use of the hands as well as the feet. As such, it was more like an early form of rugby, from which American-style football developed. William and Count Albemarle decided to get up two teams for a match, and wagered with each other on the outcome. Albemarle's team won, but William enjoyed the match so much that he canceled the royal ban against soccer.

Whether the royal ban was on or off, the ordinary English people continued to play the game, and by about 1800 it was generally considered acceptable. Of course, by that time it had become less rough and dangerous, and a few rules, though unwritten, were probably generally adhered to.

Meanwhile, Britain being the major colonial power in the world in the early 1800s, the game was being introduced into other parts of the world. Native inhabitants of these areas learned the game from British soldiers and sailors and adopted the game, in some cases because it was very similar to games they already played, in other cases because it was attractive to them.

In Spain, at first the game was suspect as being a threat to bullfighting, but gradually soccer gained popularity. In Latin America it spread inland from the coastal ports, especially those of Brazil, and while dark-skinned Brazilians could not play on official fields, they practiced and developed their skills on the beaches and back areas. Alexander Watt, who had played soccer at Cambridge University, was a booster of the game in Argentina, although a few early allowances had to be made for Argentine *macho* customs. The team of students that played in a game he had organized were arrested by the police for wearing short pants!

Back in Britain, between about 1800 and 1850, even the upper classes were beginning to play soccer. It was being played in some of the "public schools," which are comparable to U.S. private schools, among them Rugby School. In 1823, a Rugby student named William Ellis broke the no-hands rule of traditional football, or soccer, by picking up the ball and running with it. Spectators and fellow teammates thought it was very exciting to see Ellis running with the ball, and a new game was born. It became known as rugby, after the English "public school" where it began. And it was this game of rugby that North Americans later developed into American-style football.

Meanwhile, the game we know as soccer continued to attract the interest of the English upper classes, and by about 1850 it was being played in the best English "public schools," and by the most important English universities, Oxford and Cambridge. The game played at these schools differed slightly from that of the working people, since it was governed by fairly strict rules. In 1862, J. D. Thring drew up ten rules of the game that still govern modern soccer, but the official birthdate of soccer is generally acknowledged to be October 26, 1863, when the Football Association was formed.

In the meantime, the game itself was going through some changes. Many in the British upper classes, now that these upper classes had adopted the game, wanted it to be a game for "gentlemen," not played for money. Those in the nongentlemanly classes, among whom the game had become popular enough to support paid teams of workmen and craftsmen on their days off, wanted the sport to be not an amateur but a professional one. The two attitudes might have coexisted if the two types of players had not decided to compete against each other. Graduates of Cambridge and Oxford, or Rugby and Eton, could have played only against each other. And teams of weavers and other craftsmen from towns like Derby and Blackburn could have played only against each other. But under the by-laws of the Football Association, both upper-class and working-class teams could belong, and could compete against each other in the Football Association Cup final. Up until 1882, the amateur teams won the Cup, but in 1883, the Blackburn Rovers, a team of craftsmen who were unofficially being paid to play the game, beat the Old Etonions, an amateur team. This shifted the scales toward paid teams, or professionalism, and in 1885 professionalism in soccer was legalized.

Meanwhile, Scotland, Ireland, and Wales, in which soccer had also become very popular, had formed their own football associations, and in 1886 an international board consisting of two members from each of these countries' associations, plus two members from the English Football Association, was formed. In the early 1890s this board added goal nets and the penalty kick to the rules of soccer.

By the early 1900s, the game was just as popular in many other European countries as it was in Great Britain, and in 1904 France, Belgium, Sweden, Spain, Holland, Denmark, and Switzerland formed the Fédération Internationale de Football Association (FIFA) (pronounced "Feefa").

At first, the British Football Association would have nothing to do with FIFA. In 1913, two representatives from FIFA were admitted to the British international board, making an eight-member body, and despite later changes, this body still makes the rules for soccer throughout the world.

In 1924, faced with the great popularity of soccer in other countries, Britain briefly associated itself with FIFA. But in 1928, when FIFA proclaimed to the International Olympic Committee that it was the true international governing body of soccer, the British Football Association cut its ties with FIFA. And when the World Cup competition was instituted in 1930, Britain, and its Football Association, did not take part. The World Cup, after many play-offs and eliminations, ended with a contest between the two remaining teams for one of the most costly trophies in any sport. Put up by Jules Rimet, president of FIFA in 1930, the cup is solid gold and is now worth well over one hundred thousand dollars.

When the World Cup competition began, world travel was expanding. International Olympic competition had been held every four years since 1896, but the World Cup was the first truly worldwide professional competition. Both Latin America and Eastern Europe were well represented in the play-offs, and Uruguay won the coveted trophy. World

War II halted World Cup competition between 1942 and 1946, but at the same time the war continued to help the spread of soccer, especially in the East, where occupying troops on both sides played the game and introduced, or reintroduced, the inhabitants to soccer.

Shiro Otani, a great Japanese soccer promoter and fan, recalled in his book *The Charm of Soccer* an incident on New Poritain Island in the South Pacific in 1943–44. Otani was then stationed with the Japanese Navy on the island, and he and other naval officials were worried about the poor morale of the inhabitants of the island. American air raids were increasing in intensity, and the inhabitants, the Kanaka, were afraid Japan would lose the war.

By chance, a Navy Japanese official observed the delight with which some Kanaka, who had found a ball, kicked it. He told Otani what he had seen, and Otani decided to organize a soccer game. He had played the game as a student and vaguely remembered the physical layout of a soccer field and the rules. He feared the Kanaka might be too afraid of the air raids to come to play in and watch a soccer game on such an open field, but he was wrong. Both players and spectators came, and the players really knew how to play the game. Since the

Kanaka had been under German rule before World War I, Otani assumed they had learned the game from the Europeans. But how they had learned soccer was not as important to Otani as their love for the game. He was impressed with soccer's worldwide influence and attraction.

After World War II was over, the popularity of soccer increased by leaps and bounds, helped first by easier, cheaper international travel than ever before, and second by increased communications, radio, and, later, television. The Soviet Union adopted the game, as did many African countries. By the mid-1960s both South Vietnam and North Korea had excellent teams. By the late 1960s there was no question that soccer was the dominant world sport, with some twenty million active players and scores of millions of fans.

Nearly one hundred teams from countries all over the world competed in the complicated elimination competition for the 1974 World Cup finals in West Germany, and one and a half billion television viewers watched the finals. In West Germany alone, there are nearly 95,000 registered teams, ranging from grade school to professional teams.

Winning a World Cup does more for national pride in most countries than any other event, and losing can be a heavy blow, particularly in Latin American countries. In Brazil, defeat can bring a long period of national mourning, for it means a terrible loss of national prestige, not to mention an equally terrible loss of pride for individual Brazilians. In 1950, Uruguay beat Brazil in the World Cup finals; just at the moment Uruguay scored the winning goal, a Brazilian fan committed suicide!

Anything that is so emotion-laden is bound to be accompanied by violence, and as the popularity of soccer has grown, so has the violence associated with it—not the violence of its players so much as that of its fans. People in North America are familiar with the riots that occur frequently at soccer games in Latin America, and many stadiums there are built so that the crowd is separated from the field by wire fences and ditches, and police patrol the stands armed with tear gas.

There was, for example, the riot in Lima, Peru, which was to date the worst riot in sports history. The amateur teams of Argentina and Peru were competing for a place in the Olympic soccer tournament. Argentina was leading, 1–0, and there were less than two minutes to play when a member of the Peruvian team made a goal that the Uruguayan referee nullified because of rough play on the part of the Peruvian team. Both Peruvian players and the crowd, mainly Peruvian as the game was being played in their capital city, Lima, protested, but the decision went unchanged. When play resumed, a spectator entered the field area and chased the referee. The police arrested the spectator. Then another spectator, a well-known Lima sports enthusiast, tried to do the same thing. He was tripped by one police officer and hit by another. The angry crowd began to throw stones and bottles at the police, who responded with tear gas. The riot was on.

Spectators smashed windows, set buildings afire, and looted nearby stores. Even those who did not engage in such acts were not safe. They tried to get out of the stadium, but the doors were closed and locked against them. Many were trampled to death. In the end, some three hundred persons were killed, and a thousand more injured—all because of one disputed soccer goal.

Three years later, the second worst riot in the history of soccer occurred in Kayseri, Turkey, during a game between two Turkish towns, Kayseri and Sivas. The two towns had a long-standing rivalry, and in 1964 a match between them had ended in a fight in the stands that resulted in the injury of eleven persons. But this was nothing compared to the riot on September 17, 1967.

Twenty minutes into the game, the Kayseri team made a goal that was disputed by the Sivas team—and by the 5,000 Sivas fans who had traveled some 110 miles to see the game. The referee, however, allowed the goal. The stands erupted with fighting between Sivas and Kayseri fans, many of whom wielded knives, pistols, and large rocks. By the time police brought the crowd under control, 41 people had been killed and another 600 injured,

Such violent spectator behavior is not confined to Latin America or the Middle East, however. In the Scottish industrial town of Glasgow, for example, the problems in Northern Ireland have often been echoed in games between Glasgow's two top teams, the Celtics, whose followers are chiefly Roman Catholic, and the Rangers, who have predominantly Protestant fans. While confrontations between the two groups of fans have never reached the violent levels of those in Latin America and Turkey, nevertheless Glasgow police have at times taken steps to prevent violence by forbidding fans to wear their team's colors, and by searching all fans entering the stadium for bottles, knives, and guns.

Small riots have occurred in Winnepeg, Canada; in Switzerland; in Stockholm, Sweden; in Budapest, Hungary; and in practically every other city or town in every country in the world where soccer is an important sport. Nobody knows why soccer fans act so violently, but the fans of a soccer team are more loyal and more united than those of any other team in any other sport in the world. And soccer teams themselves are generally more united than teams in any other sport. The members of a soccer team are not only teammates on the field but also friends off the field. Off the field they feel that they are still representatives of their team, and they wear jackets and ties of the same colors as their team uniforms. The general feeling is that it is best for a soccer player to eat three hours before a game, and it is standard practice throughout the world for soccer teammates to meet three hours before their game to partake of a standard meal: steak and toast. The beverage depends on area and nationality: wine for Latin American, Spanish, and Italian players, tea for most others. After the game, this togetherness continues. Showers are still rare outside North America, and the common practice in many countries is for the entire team to climb into one huge tub.

American professional athletes, whatever their sports, are the best paid in the world. There are exceptions, and Pelé is one of them. In 1967, he signed a contract with the Santos team of São Paulo, Brazil, for about $4,500 a month. But most Brazilian players, of course, made a fraction of that, and so did players in other countries. Up until 1961, no British player made more than about $60 per week. To soccer players around the world, it seemed grossly unfair that a star in England or in Ghana or in Uruguay, where soccer was the No. 1 sport, should make so much less than a minor player in the United States, where soccer was way behind football, baseball, basketball, or hockey in popularity.

Still, it is not the relatively high-paid North American soccer player who should be criticized for drawing a high salary. Pelé may have signed a $4.5 million contract, but the average professional U.S. or Canadian soccer player is paid much less than the average professional player in the major United States sports.

2 Soccer in North America

Soccer was played in the United States even before the country was born. It was brought from Europe, primarily from England, by the early colonists, and its history and popularity followed that of the game in England up until the Civil War. Just as in England, between 1800 and 1850, soccer became more acceptable among the upper classes and became a standard game at colleges and universities. Called *ballown,* it was played at Princeton in 1820, and it was played by Harvard freshmen and sophomores in 1827. At Yale, Amherst, and Brown, soccer was a part of their athletic program. On November 6, 1869, Princeton and Rutgers competed in a game that Rutgers won, 6–4. It is because of this game that the college football Hall of Fame has been placed at Rutgers, although it would be much more fitting for a soccer hall of fame to be built there.

The field was almost square, as is a soccer field. The ball was round, and it could not be touched by the hands. A goal counted one point. Sounds a lot closer to soccer than football.

In the 1860s after the Civil War, rugby began to enjoy popularity in the United States. It had first been introduced in Boston, and it was generally referred to as the "Boston game." The two games might have existed side by side, or soccer might have become predominant if it hadn't been for Harvard University. In 1860 Harvard's faculty had ruled against the playing of soccer, and in 1871 it voted to adopt rugby. At first, the Harvard rugby team was hard-put to find competitors. All the other colleges were playing soccer. Harvard had to go to Canada to find another rugby team.

In 1875, however, Harvard challenged Yale to a game to be played under "concessionary rules," meaning that Harvard would accept some soccer rules and Yale would accept some rugby rules. While Harvard won, the Yale team and fans were excited about the game, and so were the observers Princeton had sent to watch it. In 1876, representatives from the top universities met in Springfield, Massachusetts, to form the Intercollegiate Football Association, and soccer ceased to be played at these schools.

Meanwhile, on neighborhood and small-town fields, and in city lots, the playing of soccer went on. It was spurred, after the Civil War, by European immigrants—Scotch, Irish, English—who helped increase the popularity of the game first on the Eastern seaboard and then in the Midwest. Later, German immigrants would help spread soccer still farther.

In 1884, the American Football Association, for soccer, was founded in Newark, New Jersey, to set standards and rules. But neither the AFA nor any of the teams it represented was rich enough to send players to England to compete with British teams. In Canada, meanwhile, soccer was also growing slowly, and in 1888 she sent a team to England.

By the early 1900s, increased immigration from Eastern European countries was helping to spread soccer still farther, and U.S. players became correspondingly better at the game. They were still not up to the standards of most of the rest of the world, however, and certainly no competition for British teams. Beginning in 1904, English teams toured the large U.S. cities and won almost every game. But these defeats caused U.S. soccer players and fans to become more determined than ever to improve the game in this country. In 1914, the United States Football Association (USFA) was formed and officially recognized by FIFA, signaling the formal entry of the United States into the most popular international sport of the day.

It wasn't exactly a widely heralded event in the United States as a whole, but it was loudly applauded in the urban ethnic neighborhoods where soccer was *the* most popular game, and where the immigrant workers who formed factory-supported teams, and their children, followed closely the progress of these teams. In the summer of 1975, all the speculation about what Pelé would do to put U.S. soccer "on the map" inspired a seventy-five-year-old resident of Brooklyn, New York, named Roy Skelly to remind the readers of the New York *Times* that soccer in the United States had been on some Americans' maps for quite some time. He told of how, sixty years before in South Brooklyn, "all the kids were nuts about soccer." They went to games between the Bethlehem Steel Team and the Robins Dry Dock team, the Todd Shipyard team and the Morse Dry Dock team, as well as games between these teams and visiting teams from Massachusetts and Rhode Island—Pawtucket and Providence, Fall River and New Bedford. They knew the trainers of the local teams, and often rode with them to games in Philadelphia, Pennsylvania, and Newark, New Jersey.

World War I slowed the progress of soccer in many parts of the world, and the United States was no exception. But when the first World Cup competition was announced for 1930, the United States managed to get together a professional team. The U.S. team did not exactly face the toughest competition there was to be had in Montevideo, Uruguay. Only four European teams entered the tournament, and England, mother country of soccer, was not represented at all. Still, it came as quite a surprise even to the American team when they beat Belgium, 3–0, in their first game and placed third in the finals.

Back home, however, professional soccer wasn't too popular. And when in 1941 the executive secretary of the United States Football Association died, interest in professional soccer was so low that the USFA did not have enough money to hire a replacement. The new executive secretary, Joe J. Barriskill, served without pay and financed the organization's operations himself for two years.

By 1950, World Cup competition had resumed, and England entered the tournament for the first time. The United States sent a team to the tournament made up of the best players from St. Louis; Chicago; Philadelphia and Pittsburgh; Fall River, Massachusetts; and New York. The tournament was held in Brazil that year. When the U.S. team learned that they would be pitted against the English team in the preliminaries, the U.S. team openly admitted they had no chance of coming up with a tie game, let alone winning—for England was one of the early favorites to win the over-all championship.

The game was played on June 29, 1950, in Belo Horizonte, Brazil. The stands were packed, and there was a sizable delegation of English fans. U.S. fans were not very well represented. Nearly everyone in the audience expected England to win, and that went for the members of both teams as well. Perhaps that was the problem; perhaps the English team was too confident. Whatever the problem, the English had plenty of chances to score a goal and didn't. The U.S. team had exactly one real chance to score a goal and did, five minutes before half time. The U.S. team beat England in what has been called, especially by the English, "football's most unbelievable result."

In later games against other teams in that World Cup series, England was beaten once more, and the U.S. team was beaten twice, both teams thus being eliminated from the tournament. The English team went home in great embarrassment. The U.S. team returned to their country triumphant, but only in their hometowns did they receive a hero's welcome.

Still, interest in soccer began very slowly to increase, as more top European and Latin American teams visited the United States, playing exhibition games with teams in various cities. While those who attended these games as spectators continued to be primarily what sportswriters commonly refer to as "ethnics," first- or second-generation immigrants, here and there more "Americanized" citizens attended and were educated in the fine points of the game.

The popularity of soccer received considerable impetus in the 1960s from two chief sources. One source, strangely enough was American-style football. By the early 1960s television had become a fixture in American homes and was helping to spread the popularity of football. The number of professional football teams increased, as did the number of high school and college teams. But football is an expensive sport. Equipment alone—helmets, special jerseys and shoes, and shoulder pads and other protectors—was beyond the budgets of many schools and towns. Also, football can be a dangerous sport, and in some communities there was strong resistance to football as a high school or grammar school sport. Casting about for an alternative fall sport, many of these communities and institutions turned to soccer.

Within a few years, even colleges that maintained

football teams were feeling pressured to add soccer to their athletic rosters. For one thing, their incoming freshman rolls were beginning to include more and more high school soccer stars. Naturally, it was a shame not to utilize that talent. Then, too, the 1960s saw an increase in the number of foreign exchange students attending U.S. colleges and universities. As soccer was the most popular sport elsewhere in the world, and as many of these foreign students, too, had soccer talent, this was all the more reason to establish soccer as a fall sport.

Once institutions began graduating talented soccer players in considerable numbers, businessmen started creating professional teams for them to play on. By the mid-1960s, the United States Football Association had become the United States Football Soccer Association and was paying its executive secretary a respectable salary. And a new organization had been founded, the National Professional Soccer League.

In 1967, professional soccer began in earnest, with the creation of two full-fledged pro soccer leagues in the United States, the National Professional Soccer League (NPSL) and the United States Soccer Association (USSA). The original United States Football Association, later the United States Football Soccer Association, had finally dropped the word *Football* from its name altogether.

While some of the prime movers behind these two leagues were real soccer fans, in truth it must be said that more were real money fans. By 1967, professional sports had become a big-money industry. Mainly due to television, fortunes were being made in professional team sports. Such fortunes are still being made. Since the mid-1960s hockey has grown tremendously in popularity and has added an additional and successful league. The same thing has happened in basketball. Football has also become so popular that new teams are being added to the National Football League. There is now professional team tennis.

For most of these sports, the task of televising games has presented no problem. Soccer involved difficulties. There were things about the game that just did not lend themselves very well to American television—for example, the lack of breaks or time-outs in a soccer game. Except in the event of serious injury, or when the ball was kicked out of bounds, or when a foul was called, there were no breaks, except at half time. And most of these breaks were very brief. Where in the world could the commercials be placed? In the United States, except for public and pay television, there is no television without commercials.

During the 1967 season, the National Professional

Soccer League was charged with false fouls and overlong delays due to minor injuries—all in order to allow time for television commercials. Obviously, that was not going to work. The decision, in the end, was to pack in as many commercials as possible before the game, at the half, and after the game.

Other changes television made necessary involved the referee's uniform (a dark shirt and shorts looked just like a regular player's colored uniform on black-and-white television) and a better idea of the time left in a half or a game (in most countries, neither players nor spectators know when the period is almost over; for television, and for U.S. fans in general, countdown clocks on electric scoreboards were used). Finally, the traditional tie game was modified. U.S. fans like a "clean decision" —one team wins and one team loses. As in football, provision was made for overtime play in the event of a tie at the end of regulation play, giving a better chance of a nontied game.

Despite such changes for the sake of increased television exposure, television coverage was not extensive. By 1968, the NPSL and the USSA, unable to make a go of it as two separate leagues, had merged to form one league, the North American Soccer League, consisting of seventeen teams. A year later, all but five had folded. Average attendance at games was thirty-three hundred. This was *not* big-money business. Perhaps there was just no way soccer was going to catch on in the United States.

A former British soccer player, Phil Woosman, became the new commissioner of the North American Soccer League in 1969. He persuaded the remaining teams to schedule their seasons from April to August, so they would not be competing with the seasons of most other major sports, especially the fall football games. He recruited overseas teams to play exhibition games, and overseas players to join U.S. teams once their home seasons were over. NASL players were not paid much money by U.S. standards—some got only three thousand dollars per season—but they were encouraged to, and they did, go into community recreation centers and high schools to drum up interest in the game.

These efforts paid off. In Dallas, when the pro team started in 1967, there were only about five hundred kids playing soccer; by the early summer of 1975 there were forty thousand. In 1969, in North America, five professional teams were playing to an average crowd of a little over three thousand per game. In 1973, nine teams were playing, and the average game was drawing sixty-two hundred fans per game. In 1974, there were fifteen teams, and some of the crowds were larger than those at major-league baseball games.

Yet the status of soccer in North America (the NASL includes two Canadian teams) was still far lower than that of the other major spectator sports, and there was still no comparison of its popularity between North America and England. By early 1975 the NASL had twenty teams and a total yearly attendance of just over one million (pro football games, by contrast, attracted twelve million to fifteen million). There were ninety-two professional British Football League clubs by early 1975, whose games drew between twenty-five million and thirty million fans. In Brazil, Italy, and the Soviet Union, the statistics were even more impressive than in Britain.

Something else was needed to fan the growing flame of North American soccer, and in 1975 the New York team, the Cosmos, took the initiative. In signing Pelé, the Cosmos hoped not only to boost attendance at their own games, but also to promote interest in American soccer in general. Whatever the result for North American soccer, Pelé himself will go down in history as one of the most important athletes the world has ever known.

Part Two
Pelé

3 Early Years

"I came from nothing," Pelé once said, and though it is not the opinion of this author that *anyone* ever comes from *nothing,* the circumstances of Pelé's birth and his early childhood did not exactly forecast stardom of any sort. At least the practical-minded would say so. Pelé's father, however, was not one of the practical-minded. The first time he saw his son he bent over to examine the newborn's skinny little legs. "Look at his legs," Dondinho do Nascimento said. "He is going to be a great soccer player."[1]

Like any other mother, particularly a first-time mother, Dondinho's wife, Celeste, also hoped that her firstborn would grow up to be *somebody,* but she had other careers in mind besides soccer. In fact, *any* other career would do. To Celeste do Nascimento that infernal sport, soccer, was to blame for the couple's poor financial circumstances, for the fact that their first child was born in an old brick house, the paint on its doors and windows cracked and crumbling, in one of the poorest sections of the poor town of Tres Coracoes in the Brazilian state of Minas Gerais.

Dondinho do Nascimento was a soccer player, and a very good one. But there were many "very good" soccer players in Brazil, and unless a man was lucky enough or talented enough to play for a team in one of the large cities, he could not make a living at it.

The difficulty in making a living playing soccer was not the only reason for the do Nascimentos' poverty. There was a racial reason as well. Dondinho do Nascimento was very dark, and thus it was difficult for him to enjoy the same rights and opportunities as lighter-skinned Brazilians.

Back in the 1600s and 1700s, European countries had claimed and colonized the various areas of Latin America. The officials they sent to rule the colonies, and the colonists they sent to lay claim to the land, were white. They took land from the brown-skinned Indians and established themselves as their rulers. They built plantations, and soon there were not enough native Latin Americans willing to work on them. So the European colonists imported

African slaves for the purpose. Over the years, the three groups, the white European colonists, the Indians, and the Africans mingled, and through intermarriage the various races blended to a certain extent, so that by the beginning of the 1900s Brazilians, for example, spanned the range of skin colors, from white to black. Rights and privileges were accorded largely on the basis of skin color; the lighter one's complexion, the more rights and privileges one enjoyed. These divisions along racial lines continued even after Brazil and other Latin American countries achieved their independence. And with the United States strongly influencing these countries in the first half of the twentieth century, there was little change in this social policy. Growing up in the 1920s and 1930s Dondinho do Nascimento had to contend not only with poverty but also with discrimination. The two combined prevented him from getting the kind of education he needed to get a well-paying job. And while there were no formal, written rules barring dark-skinned players from the big-city soccer teams, or the Brazilian national team, the fact was that there were no dark-skinned players on these teams. Thus, while Dondinho had great hope for his first son, the little boy had a lot against him from birth. Not only was he born into a poor family, but also he was as dark as his father.

Pelé was born Edson Arantes do Nascimento on October 23, 1940, in the small town whose name in English means "Three Hearts," in the southeastern part of Brazil. He was his parents' firstborn, although soon he would be joined by a brother, Zoca, and a sister, Maria Lucia. And while the do Nascimentos welcomed each child, Celeste do Nascimento, particularly, wondered how in the world they were going to manage with another mouth to feed.

Playing in a small town like Tres Coracoes, Dondinho did not make very much money, and he held odd jobs as well to try to support his family. Meanwhile, he hoped to get a chance to play for a big soccer club in a large city like São Paulo or Rio.

Early in 1942, he received such a chance. He was invited to play for the Atletico Mineiro team in the city of Belo Horizonte. Excited and hopeful, he left his family to travel to the city and show the team what he could do. He was confident of his ability, and was already making plans to send for his family when he went into his first game with the Atletico Mineiro team. However, this was not to be his big chance at all. In that very first game, Dondinho do Nascimento suffered a serious knee injury. He returned to Tres Coracoes in pain and depres-

Pelé could be a ballet dancer or a gymnast, as he does a calisthenics routine during a workout with the New York Cosmos. Medical experts have taken numerous measurements and done many tests to determine what makes Pelé so much better than other soccer stars. These experts have concluded that he would have been a "genius" in whatever sport he chose. *(Wide World Photos)*

Pelé completes an excellent pass to Santos teammate Alfonso in a 1972 exhibition game in San Francisco. Santos beat Universidad de Mexico 5–1. *(Wide World Photos)*

It looks like midair fisticuffs, but in reality Pelé has just headed the ball away from his Toronto Metros opponent in his second game as a New York Cosmos player. Although he did not score himself, Pelé directed his team to a 2–0 win in the regulation league game. *(Wide World Photos)*

In his first game with the Cosmos, Pelé thrilled the crowd at New York's Downing Stadium with his masterful moves. Here, maintaining complete control of the ball, he leaps over an opponent. *(Wide World Photos)*

Pelé is all alone with the ball in his first game with the Cosmos, and it is unlikely that his Dallas Tornado opponents will be able to take it away. His left-foot kicks are legendary in soccer. *(United Press International Photo)*

When the Santos team played exhibition games in the United States, many who otherwise did not attend soccer games would turn out to see the great Pelé play. A record crowd in Oakland, California, came to see him in August 1968. He scored two goals to lead Santos to a 3–1 victory over the Oakland Clippers. *(Wide World Photos)*

Pelé does a flip in the air as he kicks the ball back over his head in a game in September 1968. No wonder he loses 4–5 pounds per game! *(Wide World Photos)*

sion to tell his wife, who was pregnant with their second child, that he would be unable to play soccer or to do any strenuous work for a while.

A few months later, Zoca was born, and shortly after that Dondinho, whose knee had healed, received an invitation to play with the Hipacre club in the city of Lorena. He fared better with this team, and shortly he moved his family to the city, for his wife did not like him being away so much of the time and he disliked traveling back and forth. When the family moved, Pelé was not quite two years old, and so he remembers little of his birthplace. Nor does he remember much about Lorena, although he later learned from his parents that it was at Lorena that his father's soccer skills received their first real exposure. He became famous in the Lorena area for the way he was able to hit the ball with his head.

Still, Dondinho was not making enough playing soccer to support his family. In Lorena, too, he worked at odd jobs on the side and hoped for an invitation to play with a team that paid higher salaries. It was for this reason that he changed clubs about a year later and moved his family to the city of São Lourenço.

Dondinho's and Celeste's third child and first daughter, Maria Lucia, was born there. A year later, Dondinho decided to change clubs again, which naturally meant another move. Pelé was four years old by then, old enough to be aware of the life around him. He heard his mother complain about constantly moving, about leading a gypsylike life. He heard his father insist that this was really a big break, and that he had been offered a public, or city worker's job, as well as a position on a soccer team in the city of Bauru. Why, his new team, the Bauru Athletic Club, would even pay for the family's train tickets to the city. Of course, Celeste do Nascimento assented. She wanted to believe in her husband.

That first train ride remains one of Pelé's most vivid childhood memories, and the city of Bauru was the first place he lived that he was old enough to really notice and remember. They lived in a neighborhood full of children, and Pelé and Zoca spent their days playing in the streets. Their mother worried about them, especially about little Zoca, although Pelé was a very responsible older brother. He insisted that he and Zoca would be all right and that they wanted to play with their friends. Perhaps Celeste do Nascimento, in her angrier moments, reminded her oldest son that it was unlikely their family would be in Bauru very long. The public job that Dondinho had expected had not materialized, and his salary from the Bauru Athletic Club (BAC) was just not enough to feed a growing family.

On the day that the public job did come through for Dondinho do Nascimento, the family rejoiced as Pelé could not remember it had done before. Certainly there had been happiness and celebration when his father had played a very good soccer game, but such occasions did not compare with the celebration of his getting a steady job. His mother laughed and smiled. Now they would be able to stay in one place, take care of themselves, and raise the kids. While he did not really understand it at the time, this occasion made a definite impact on Pelé. Years later, when he began to make good money from soccer, he would save it and invest it, so that when he had a wife and children he would never have to subject them to an uncertain life.

Those were happy days for Pelé, who was too young to work or to go to school. He played all day with the children his age in the neighborhood. He liked the afternoons and weekends best, for it was then that the older boys were out of school and playing soccer. Pelé and his friends would watch the older boys and dream of growing older and playing soccer, too. When he was not watching the older boys play soccer or playing with his friends, he would go to the nearby airfield and watch the airplanes there take off and land. His main ambition was to be a great soccer player, just like his father, but he was not yet of school age, and so he saw no reason why he could not be a great pilot as well.

At last the time came for Pelé to start school. He looked forward to going to school, for it meant he would be one of the big boys. At first, he was very quiet in school, listening to and watching his teacher, his classmates. Everything was strange and new and exciting. But after a while the newness wore off. Pelé was bored. He disliked sitting in one place all day, and listening, listening. As time went on, he spent more time gazing out the window and thinking about what he would do after school than he did paying attention to what was going on in class.

Now that he was in school, Pelé felt he should be allowed to play soccer with the big boys. But every time he tried to get into their games, he was sent back to the sidelines. He was too young, they said. Pelé and the other boys his age resented this exclusion. They were sure they could play better than many of the older boys. Out of spite, they disturbed the older boys' games as often as they could. Their favorite trick was to wait for the ball to come near where they sat watching, and to get up and kick it as hard and as far away as they could!

Eventually, Pelé and his friends grew tired of giving the older boys a hard time and decided to organize their own games. The only equipment they needed was a ball, and like countless boys in countless cities, they collected old socks to make one. At last, they had their ball and were ready for their first game.

"I'll never forget that afternoon," Pelé recalls. "That was our team, and I was very proud. But everybody wanted to give orders and tell the others what to do. We had so much shouting in the first game that we started having complaints from the neighbors, and eventually my mother heard them and I was punished."[2]

Of course, that did not stop either Pelé or his friends from pursuing their soccer "careers." For Pelé, soccer became much more important than school. So did watching the planes take off and land at the nearby airfield. In fact, just about anything became more important to Pelé than school, although soccer and aviation were his particular loves. By the time he was in second grade, Pelé was cutting classes as often as he could and had become one of the "bad boys" in the school.

On some days, he and some of the other "hooky players" went to the airfield instead of to school. As it was not a large field, much time passed between the arrivals or takeoffs of the planes. In between, when there was no action on the field, Pelé and his friends played nearby. One day, Pelé remembers, they were playing near the field and one of the kids called to them to look at something very strange. A plane had crashed nearby, and a dead man had been carried to the airport. Pelé watched, stunned, as a doctor and other men bent over the body. When finally Pelé looked for his friends, nobody was there. He ran. He ran until he got home in tears and was so scared that never again did he want to think about being an aviator.

He took up swimming instead. There was no swimming pool in the neighborhood, so the kids swam in the nearby river. The only trouble was, the river had a very strong current, and one had to be a very good swimmer in order not to get into trouble. Pelé was taught to swim by Zinho, the strongest boy and the best swimmer in the group with which he hung out.

One day, Zinho decided that the group should go swimming, and of course everybody went because nobody wanted to get beaten up by Zinho. Pelé, who was still not a very skilled swimmer, although he would not admit it, remained close to Zinho. He would grab onto Zinho's feet, and Pelé would kick as hard as he could while Zinho moved his arms and pulled him along. Suddenly, the two young swimmers encountered a strong undertow, and Pelé's hands slipped from his friend's legs.

Pelé panicked and began thrashing about in the water. Zinho swam back to help him, but there is no one stronger than a drowning swimmer. Little Pelé grabbed the older boy and almost drowned him too! Luckily, a passing stranger heard the other boys' cries for help. He found a long branch and held it out so they could grab onto it. Tired and shaken, the two boys collapsed on the riverbank.

This experience did not make Pelé afraid of the water, but he learned to swim very well *close* to the riverbank before he again ventured out into the deep water.

By the time Pelé was in third grade, he absolutely hated school. He had had the same teacher for first and second grade, and she had been very lenient about his frequent absences and about his lack of attention to his classwork. But for third grade he had a different teacher, and she took quite a different attitude toward him. Whenever he was absent, she reported him which got him in trouble with the principal as well as with his mother. And when he acted up in class, his teacher would think up punishments to embarrass him. The most embarrassing times were when she would make him kneel on hard beans in front of the class. This was most uncomfortable, but Pelé still did not learn his lesson. Instead, whenever the teacher wasn't looking, he would remove one of the beans and put it in his pocket, or elsewhere on the floor. Soon, he would have moved all the beans, much to the delight of his snickering classmates. He exasperated his teacher. Instead of being embarrassed, he used her punishments as an opportunity to entertain the class!

Naturally, when school was dismissed, Pelé was usually the first one out of the classroom. He was free! He would not have to go back to school until the next morning. As he grew older, he was given homework assignments, but despite his mother's constant efforts, he rarely did them. One day she caught him before he went out, and forbade him to leave until he had finished his homework. He was very angry with her at the time, but later he would be extremely grateful that she had kept him inside.

Some construction work was being done near his house, and it was one of the favorite sites for Pelé and his friends to play. They would dig caves in the huge mounds of soft dirt, spending hours hollowing out the caves and playing in them. They enjoyed doing this most when it was raining, for then they would play in the warm, dry caves while the rain poured down outside.

It was raining on the day that Pelé's mother made him stay inside, and he was very unhappy. He looked at his homework, but his mind was on the fun the others must be having out at the construction site. Last time he had been there, they had built a particularly nice cave. If it was still there, they would surely be having a great time playing in it.

Suddenly, he heard one of his friends calling his name. The cave they had built had collapsed from the rain, the friend reported breathlessly, and a boy was trapped inside! Pelé rushed to the construction site with his friend and joined the crowd of onlookers who had gathered to watch the people who were digging frantically, trying to reach the boy before he suffocated. But when at last they found him, the boy was dead. Pelé cried for hours. He felt so guilty, for he had helped to build the cave. He was also very frightened, for he realized that the boy trapped in the collapsed cave could very well have been himself.

As time went on, Pelé's respect for his father's soccer talent grew. Dondinho do Nascimento was still playing with the Bauru Athletic Club (BAC), and

Pelé went to as many games as he could. He watched every kick and every move his father made. At home, he was constantly after his father to explain a play or demonstrate a move, and his mother complained that Pelé was becoming a soccer fanatic.

She had reason to say this. Pelé's grandmother, Ambrosina, lived with the family, and as the house was very small, Pelé, his little brother, Zoca, and his grandmother all slept in the same room. Zoca slept by himself on a small bed, and Pelé and his grandmother shared the larger bed. On many nights, Pelé's grandmother would discover that Pelé had gone to bed with a soccer "ball" made of newspapers and old socks. She would chuckle and remove the ball from his hands, putting it under the bed. But in the morning, Pelé's mother would not think it funny at all that her elder son had gone to bed with a soccer "ball."

In 1950, the Brazilian national team was in World Cup play, and the final, championship game between Brazil and Uruguay was carried on Brazilian radio, the tournament being held in Brazil. Dondinho, Pelé, and Zoca gathered around the radio, listening intently, while Celeste prepared dinner in the kitchen. When Brazil made a goal, Pelé ran to the kitchen to inform his mother that their team would surely win. But later Uruguay made a goal and eventually won the World Cup. Dondinho and Zoca were crestfallen, and Pelé began to cry. "Do you see what soccer has done to all of you, Dondinho?" Celeste demanded. "It has made you suffer, and now it is making your son suffer."[3]

That night in bed Pelé could not sleep for thinking about that World Cup game. He was devastated about Brazil's loss, and he determined that when he grew up his country would never lose again. For days afterward all he talked about was what he would do for the Brazilian national team when he grew up. Celeste do Nascimento worried about having another "dreamer" in the family. But her husband reminded her that their son could be getting into trouble in the streets instead. After all, what could happen to him in a soccer game?

Once, something almost did happen at one of the BAC games. Dondinho was playing particularly well that day, and Pelé beamed with pride as he listened to the crowd applaud and shout in appreciation. Then Pelé heard someone near him cry, "Dondinho, you lousy player, go home, you bum!"

In a rage, Pelé picked up a brick and challenged the man, who was twice his size, prepared to fight him unless he took back what he had said about his father. Fortunately for Pelé, one of his father's friends stepped in and warned the man not to touch the youngster. But then, the two men began to fight, and soon the entire section of spectators was hitting and punching in a brawl that most did not even know had started when a little boy had tried to defend his father.

Back at home after the game, Dondinho, who had learned of the incident, had a serious talk with his boy. He told him that in sports you have to get used to people saying things they don't really mean, that the only way to keep them happy is to do your best to score and never pay attention to those criticisms. And Pelé always followed his advice, and admired him more and more for everything he was.

Pelé wondered why his father did not get to play for a big club. After all, in Pelé's opinion, his father was the greatest soccer player ever. But Dondinho explained that talent was not enough. One must also have luck. He had not been very lucky; he had injured his knee, and at times it prevented him from playing as well as he might.

By the time Pelé was in junior high school, he and his friends were so involved in soccer and played so often that they thought of little else. They played all day on weekends and after school. They played on the streets, and as they had no other way to mark boundary lines, those who had shoes took them off and used them to mark the boundaries.

Others did not have shoes, and so everyone played barefoot. When darkness came, they continued to play by the glow of the street lights. Sometimes they got into trouble, especially when they kicked the ball too high and it hit the electrical wires, causing them to short-circuit and black out the neighborhood.

But Pelé and his friends, who included his younger brother, Zoca, would not let anything deter them from playing soccer, and eventually they decided to form a team. They named it after a street in their neighborhood, Rua Sete de Setembro (September 7 Street). It was the logical street name to choose, for September 7 is a national holiday in Brazil, commemorating the date in 1882 when Brazil declared its independence from Portugal. Then they set about acquiring uniforms and a real ball. By taking up a collection among their relatives and friends, and by collecting and selling empty bottles and cans, they managed to raise enough money for their shorts, shirts, and socks. They could not afford the proper shoes, but they could get by with other shoes. What they really needed was a ball. It was expensive, and they just could not come up with the money for it. One of the national magazines was running a contest in which a regular soccer ball was offered as a prize to anyone who could fill an album with photographs of some twenty famous soccer players. Some pictures were easy to get, but others were very hard to find. However, the members of the 7 de Setembro team realized they could not get a ball any other way. They managed to get even the so-called impossible-to-get pictures, and at last they had their ball.

Now that they had a team, and most of the proper equipment, they needed competition. Many times when they played in the evening or on weekends they had a sizable audience of city workers who, after they had finished for the day, would gather to watch the boys play. So the team invited the workers to form their own team and to play against them. The workers eagerly agreed, and while they played in their work clothes and always lost, they enjoyed the games immensely. Meanwhile, the 7 de Setembro team was getting much-needed practice.

As time passed, the team became a strong one and began to enjoy a reputation in Bauru. Each section of the city had a youth team, and Pelé's team began to receive challenges to play the youth teams from other parts of Bauru. They were called the "Barefeeted," because word had gotten around about how they used to play barefoot and how they did not have the proper shoes. But even after they raised the money to buy regulation shoes, the name stuck. It was at about this time also that Pelé received his nickname, although no one knows why. All of a sudden everyone was calling him Pelé. Personally, he liked his real name, Edson, better, or even the nickname his family called him, "Dico"; but he realized that it was good to have a nickname that people would remember, and obviously people remembered the nickname "Pelé."

Pelé and his team became very well known in Bauru. They were scrappers, and they always played as if their lives depended on winning each game. They began to attract crowds, and even Dondinho do Nascimento, who was always very busy either working or playing himself, managed to attend a few games. Whenever he did, he offered advice to his son and the other boys. This advice was very important to the team, for they had no adult to coach them. Pelé, of course, was particularly lucky, for he had many more opportunities to receive advice from his father than the others did. To the best of his ability, Pelé passed on this advice to his teammates, for he understood that soccer is a team game and that a team goes nowhere if it relies on one or two stars and does not encourage the contributions of all its players.

However, Pelé had become something of a star on his team, and he was becoming personally well known throughout the city. He received invitations to play with youth teams in other sections of the city, which did not mean he had to leave his own team. He simply loaned himself out to other teams at times when his own team was not playing. It was in such a situation that he received his first "contract." Across the river from Pelé's neighborhood was a section of the city that Pelé and his friends considered forbidden territory. The kids over there were said to be wild, and Pelé and his friends were afraid of them. Thus, when one of the "wild" kids came to invite Pelé to play for their team for a few days, he was a little afraid of accepting. But when he heard he would be paid, he changed his mind. It was the first time he had ever been paid for playing soccer, and although the money was not great, it nevertheless meant a lot to him.

In 1952, when Pelé was twelve years old, the mayor of Bauru decided to sponsor a competition among all the youth teams from the various sections of the city. The 7 de Setembro team was very excited about the tournament, and they decided they needed a more impressive name for the team. So they changed it to Ameriquinha. Before long, they also had a real manager.

Three members of the team were brothers, and one day their father, Ze Leite, showed up and offered to manage the team. The boys eagerly accepted. At last they had an adult to lead and advise them.

Even if no adult had come forward to help them, Pelé and his teammates would have been confident going into the competition. They knew they could play well, better than many of the other teams in the city, for they had already played, and beaten, a number of them. As Pelé puts it, "We knew how to play soccer on the streets without shoes, without a professional soccer ball, and there we were playing very seriously with uniforms, shoes, and on a very comfortable field covered with beautiful grass. Why wouldn't we win? We had to."[4]

During the preliminary games of the competition, and the semifinals, they did, and then it was the afternoon of the crucial game. It seemed to the Ameriquinha team that the whole city attended that game. The stands were packed. The mayor was there, their friends and relatives were there. Pelé's father was there.

Pelé wanted so much to win for his father, to

play better than he ever had before, and he did. He moved on the field as if he knew exactly what everyone else on his own team and the opposing team would do. He "headed" the ball as skillfully as his father. His goals caused the crowd to "ooh" with awe. The Ameriquinha team won the tournament, and the crowd went wild. For the first time in his life, Pelé heard a huge crowd chanting his name: "Pe-lé, Pe-lé!" They threw money to the winning team, and the poor boys from Pelé's team scrambled to get it. But for Pelé, the most important reaction was his father's and, later, his mother's.

After the game, his father came to him. "Son, that was a great game," he said. "I loved it." They returned home together to tell his mother about the game. She smiled and hugged and kissed her son. "That was the first time I saw her happy about soccer," says Pelé.[5]

Now that Pelé was a soccer "star," he was included in the activities of the older boys in the neighborhood, those who years before had not let him play in their games. Naturally, Pelé was flattered and eager to prove that he was worthy of their attention. Thus, one day when they gathered under a tree and offered him a cigarette, he took it.

As Pelé was trying to follow his friends' instructions as to how to inhale, his father passed by. Pelé froze, hoping his father would not notice him. For his part, Dondinho do Nascimento stopped briefly, said hello to the boys, and continued on his way. Pelé knew his father had seen him smoking, and he dreaded going home.

Later, at home, Pelé's father calmly asked him why he was smoking. Pelé answered that he was just trying to learn; after all, most of his friends did. His father explained to him that if he wanted to be a good athlete he must take care of his body. However, if he was going to smoke he should buy his own cigarettes.

Pelé looked at the money his father offered him and felt very ashamed. He knew his father never drank or smoked, and he felt badly for not living up to his father's standards. He did not accept the money, and he never tried smoking again. When his friends tried to get him to smoke, he reminded them that an athlete had to take care of his health. There wasn't much they could say in answer to that.

Pelé and his team continued to develop their skills and to win games. But then they suffered a serious setback. Ze Leite decided to move his family to São Paulo, and thus, in one fell swoop, the team lost not only its "manager" but also three of its players. Discouraged, the rest of the team could not summon the morale or the spirit to reorganize their team. The Ameriquinha team disbanded. Pelé, who showed so much promise, found himself a player without a team.

4 Breaking into the Game

Pelé was lost without his team. In many ways, it had been his life, and though he spent many hours practicing his soccer skills alone or with friends, it was just not the same. He rarely went to school now, and his mother began to be very impatient with him. While he was playing on a team, and making something of a name for himself, she tried not to complain. But now things were different. He did not go to school, he no longer had a team; all he did was kick a soccer ball around. Perhaps he should get a job, she suggested. So Pelé got a job as a shoemaker's apprentice, earning two dollars a month, and hoped for some kind of break that would enable him to play team soccer again.

That break came in a very short time. The Bauru Athletic Club, on whose professional team Pelé's father played, decided to sponsor a youth team. Naturally, everyone in Pelé's neighborhood wanted to be on it, but they had to wait to be invited, and the waiting was torture. When Pelé was invited to be on the team he was overjoyed, and he accepted without question.

"It was great to belong to a professional club," he recalls. "We had everything. The whole uniform was there—if the shoes were tight, they would exchange them for us. They would do anything we wanted! It was great. I never saw my friends so obedient, listening carefully, trying their best to give a good impression."[1]

What was even greater was the news that they would have as their coach none other than Valdemar De Brito. De Brito was a legend in Brazil, a soccer star before Pelé was even born. Yet, while Pelé had never seen the retired star play, people would later note the remarkable resemblance between their soccer playing styles. Pelé would be very pleased about such comments.

At first, however, he was merely in awe of his coach, aware that he was in the presence of greatness, listening intently to every word. Dondinho do Nascimento knew De Brito very well, and he constantly reminded his son to listen to the former star's instructions. Pelé hardly had to be reminded, and it was easy to do so, for De Brito was an excellent coach with kids, kind and encouraging, but tough when it was necessary.

It did not take long for De Brito to take an interest in one of his young players in particular. Later, De Brito would say of Pelé, "Of all the players . . . only one stood out. I immediately spotted what can be called genius."[2]

Pelé recalls, "I noticed a special interest for me; one day he said, 'Kid, you have a great future ahead of you but you have a lot to learn yet.' He would correct my faults and point out my mistakes, but left me free to try my own dribbles and passes, new ways to carry the ball, etc."[3]

Before long, the BAC youth team had built a solid reputation in Bauru. In fact, their games began to attract more spectators than those of the BAC professional team, and not a few soccer fans in Bauru commented that the professional team would be better if the kids played on it rather than the regular players. Pelé did not like to hear such comments, for his father was on the BAC professional team. But Dondinho do Nascimento did not seem to mind. He was proud of his son, and pleased that he was doing so well with the BAC youth team.

Thus it came as unhappy news that Valdemar De Brito had been offered a better job in São Paulo and was going to leave Bauru. The news came as a complete surprise to Pelé, who had looked forward to several years of instruction from De Brito. Like the others on the youth team, he lost his spirit, and could not summon the morale or the energy to play as well for his new coach.

For Pelé, it was time for something new, and soon an opportunity presented itself. A well-known player from Rio de Janeiro, who had heard about Pelé, visited him and invited him to go with him to Rio. Pelé could not believe his good fortune. He was so excited that he did not take into account the reaction his parents would have to the idea.

When the player, whose name was Tim, spoke to Dondinho do Nascimento about taking Pelé to Rio, Dondinho was very pleased. But at the same time he was very doubtful. After all, Pelé was only fifteen, and Tim was suggesting a very big step for such a young boy. Dondinho also realized his wife would probably be against the idea, and he refused to give his permission before consulting his wife. As expected, she was absolutely against it, and sadly Pelé watched his "big opportunity" vanish. Needless to say, he was a bit resentful. For his part, Dondinho do Nascimento worried that he had caused his son to miss the kind of chance he had hoped for all his life and never gotten.

As it turned out, denying that opportunity only

Pelé's speed on a soccer field is unmatched, as his Guadalajara, Mexico, opponents found out when they played an exhibition game against Santos, Brazil, in Los Angeles in 1973. Even when played between two foreign teams, off-season exhibition games in which the great Pelé played drew some of the largest crowds ever to attend soccer matches in the United States. *(United Press International Photo)*

Pelé twists in midair as he drives the ball downfield past his opponent in a 1973 exhibition game between Santos, Brazil, and Guadalajara, Mexico, in Los Angeles. Santos won the game, 2–1. *(United Press International Photo)*

The "slim figure of perfection" who is the world's most famous athlete glides past his Dallas Tornado opponents before a crowd of 21,278 at Downing Stadium. The newest Cosmos player helped his team to come from behind 0–2 to tie the game at 2–2. Pelé scored one of the Cosmos' goals, and with a fine pass assisted a teammate with the other. *(United Press International Photo)*

In his first game as a member of the New York Cosmos at Downing Stadium, Pelé hops over a Dallas Tornado player as another downed Tornado looks on. Pelé, admittedly not yet in top playing shape, impressed the crowds with his all-out effort in leading his new team to a 2–2 tie. *(Wide World Photos)*

Pelé seems to dance effortlessly between his Dallas Tornado opponents in his first game with the New York Cosmos on June 15, 1975. Postgame statistics revealed that during the ninety-minute game he touched the ball seventy-six times and lost it only five times. *(United Press International Photo)*

Pelé skillfully maneuvers the
around a Washington Darts player
1970 exhibition game in the U
States. *(Wide World Photos)*

left Pelé free to accept another, greater opportunity. A few months later, Valdemar De Brito returned to Bauru, for the express purpose of taking Pelé back with him to São Paulo. The team he coached there, Santos, was looking for new talent, and in De Brito's opinion the best new talent around was the youngster he had coached on the BAC youth team in Bauru.

De Brito visited Pelé's father. While in his heart Dondinho do Nascimento was as excited for his son as he would have been if the offer had been made to him, he tried to be practical, to be a good father. Pelé was young. Wouldn't it be better for him to wait a couple more years, to gain more maturity, before he tried to make a team like Santos? But De Brito convinced him that Pelé would be better off with a team like Santos. Most of the players on the team were young, and the team took good care of its players.

But just because his father had been convinced did not mean that Pelé was on his way to Santos. Celeste do Nascimento was very much against the idea. Only after De Brito assured her that he would take care of her son did she agree. "I'll never forget her words," Pelé recalls. "'But he is still a baby,' she said; 'he must have somebody to watch over him.' Well, after everything was settled my mother started preparing my luggage and also getting me some long pants; because until that day I only wore shorts. She made a beautiful pair of long ones, and I felt very proud the day I wore them for the first time. I felt great, and I knew I was becoming a man."[4]

Pelé's father accompanied him and De Brito to São Paulo, and for Pelé this train ride would be equally as memorable as the one he had taken, years before, from São Lourenço to Bauru. Many Bauru soccer fans and Pelé's BAC team resented his going, but Pelé was not troubled by this reaction. He knew that if he was signed by the Santos team, the people of his hometown would be proud of him and boast that he had gotten his start in soccer right there in Bauru. As the train sped along, carrying him away from Bauru, Pelé gave little thought to what he was leaving. He was so excited he could hardly keep still. He was fascinated by the things he saw out the train window, and his head was full of dreams about what São Paulo and the Santos team would be like. He found it almost impossible to listen to De Brito's advice about how to act, although when he heard the older man warn him not to smoke or drink or chase after women, he assured De Brito that he did not do that sort of thing.

When they arrived in São Paulo, they went immediately to the main stadium. Santos was playing another team, Comercial, in a championship match, and De Brito had arranged for very good seats. Before long, Pelé was cheering for Santos as if he was part of the team already. After the game, De Brito took Pelé and his father to the Santos locker room, which was the scene of celebration, for the team had won the game. Pelé was introduced to the players, nearly all of whom he already felt he knew. He had studied their pictures and knew their names by heart. Vasconcelos, Lulu, Zito, Jair, Formiga, Pagao, Pepe . . . he felt very young and very small among them, and he wondered why they bothered to take the time to make him feel welcome. For his part, Dondinho do Nascimento lived the dream that had once been his, through his son.

His father returned to Bauru two days later, and Valdemar De Brito had business elsewhere in São Paulo. Thus Pelé was all alone when he first scrimmaged with the team. "I felt scared and lonely," he recalls, ". . . because I was left alone with all those 'tigers.'"[5] Back in Bauru, he had heard that the players on the Santos team, like most professionals, would make it rough for him, would not help him. And thus, during that first scrimmage, he lacked confidence and was afraid he would make a mistake.

"I couldn't do much because I was nervous," says Pelé, "but little by little I gained confidence and was even asking for passes and trying to dribble to score. At the end they were all impressed enough to say something nice, which made me feel great and very confident. They were different from what I had heard in Bauru."[6]

It was not long before the president of the Santos club offered Pelé a contract. Naturally, Pelé would have signed without question, if the matter had been up to him alone. But it was not. He had to consult with his parents first. So, with Valdemar De Brito, he returned to Bauru.

Dondinho do Nascimento agreed right away. But both Pelé's mother and grandmother objected to his being so far away from them. They cried, and seeing their sorrow, Pelé cried, too. He did not want to hurt them. He wouldn't sign the contract; he would stay home as they wished. But Valdemar would not take "No" for an answer. Once again he visited the do Nascimento household and explained at length how important this opportunity was for Pelé. And once again he managed to convince even Celeste do Nascimento that signing with the Santos team was her son's big opportunity to become a real soccer professional.

Thus, Pelé returned to São Paulo with Valdemar De Brito. Almost immediately, he signed the contract with Santos. Under its terms he would be paid about $120 per month, and room and board would be free.

Once again Pelé's life would be soccer. He spent hours working out at the stadium, sometimes with his team, sometimes with a teammate or two or all alone. When he was not playing soccer, he would go to a movie or to the beach with fellow teammates. Once in a while, he would go to a nearby bar to kill time, but as he neither drank nor smoked, he did not feel a part of the bar's clientele. More and more, his free-time thoughts were on soccer, how he could improve, how he could move the ball in more imaginative ways.

Gradually, as he gained more experience, his soccer game improved. When he was first signed to the Santos club, he was placed on the defensive team. One day, quite by accident, he found himself "on the front," and he played so well on the attack that the coach decided to keep him there. That was fine with Pelé. He felt much better and freer on offense. Meanwhile, contrary to what he had heard back in Bauru, his teammates continued to be friendly to him and to help him. They gave him advice, shared with him the benefit of their own experience. He listened and learned. They even gave him advice about his activities off the field. They reminded him that a career in soccer was really a very short one, and if he was smart he would save his money and provide for himself in the years after his career was over. Pelé took their advice. His own expenses were minimal, and so he sent most of his salary home to his father, who in turn invested it for him in order that he might have a secure future.

A year passed. Pelé was now a starter on the Santos team. He was sixteen years old, and in that year he had what he calls his first "official big game." It was against the AIK team from Sweden, in Santos' home stadium in São Paulo. Pelé played remarkably well for a sixteen-year-old, and while the Swedish team was tougher than he had expected, his team won.

Other big games would follow, and because of the number of goals he scored, Pelé would be named Athlete of the Year. He began to be recognized on the streets of São Paulo, to see his picture on magazine covers at the newstands he passed. Newspaper articles on the Santos games carried his name and his picture. Many youngsters in his position would have become conceited, have developed "an attitude." Not Pelé. "I was still the same Pelé from the streets of Bauru," he says.[7]

Brazilian writer Benedito Ruy Barbosa, who has

published a book about Pelé, first met the soccer star when he was barely seventeen but already famous around São Paulo. At that time, Barbosa was a reporter for the newspaper *Ultima Hora,* and he was seeking an interview with the exciting young player.

"Where did you come from?" Barbosa asked.

"From Bauru," Pelé answered. "I'm Dondinho's son!"

"Which Dondinho?" Barbosa asked in a puzzled voice.

Pelé's smile disappeared; he was obviously disappointed. "Are you a sportswriter?" he demanded.

Barbosa assured him he was.

"And you don't know Dondinho, my father?"[8]

While the interview was supposed to be about Pelé, Pelé spoke more about his father than about himself—how Dondinho was the greatest and would have been able to prove it if only he had not been injured. Barbosa was highly impressed with the youth's modesty and love for his father.

When the regular season was over, Pelé returned home for a rest, although so many friends and relatives came to visit him that he did not rest as much as he had expected. Meanwhile, an important match was scheduled between the Brazilian National Team and that of Argentina. The prize was the "Rocca Cup," a very coveted prize in Latin America.

The Brazilian National Team was made up of the best players from all the professional teams across the country. Pelé's supporters told him he would be chosen, but he did not think so. After all, he was only sixteen, and he knew of so many great players. He could not picture himself as one of the handful of "best players" in Brazil. Shortly, however, he was to change his perspective.

He was at home one day, listening to the radio, when he heard the announcer give the list of players who had been chosen for the Brazilian National Team. He listened with interest as he heard the names, for he either knew or knew of every one of them. Catilho, Gilmar, Dialma, Nilton Santos . . . He listened to the names and nodded or shook his head as he thought how good they were. Then the announcer listed the names on the reserve team: Mazzola, Pelé . . . Pelé! He was so excited that he wanted to shout out the news. Instead, he stood stock still, shaking all over. He had been named to the National Team, and he was so nervous he couldn't move.

Even his father could not believe it at first. He asked his son if he was sure he had heard his name. But when friends and neighbors began to converge on the house to congratulate Pelé, Dondinho knew Pelé had indeed heard his own name on the radio. He asked his son if he was nervous, and Pelé nodded that indeed he was. He was nervous as he traveled to Maracaña Stadium in Rio de Janeiro, and as he scrimmaged with the other chosen players as they prepared for the tournament. But gradually he grew calmer. After all, he was only on the reserve team. The way the men on the starting team were playing in scrimmage, perhaps he would not play at all.

Pelé was especially calm on the first day of the tournament, for he was quite sure he would not play that day. He was sitting on the bench, watching the game, when the manager rushed up to him and ordered him over to the first-aid area for a leg massage. To Pelé this could only mean that he was indeed going to play. He was, the coach confirmed. Watching the game as his legs were massaged to get him ready, Pelé determined to put on a good showing. This was the first such chance he'd ever had.

When Pelé entered the game, the score was 1–0 in favor of Argentina. The Argentinians had a strong team, but in Pelé's opinion the Brazilian team had much more style; they simply had not had a chance to display it. As they raced up and down the field,

Pelé looked for an opportunity to make or to set up a goal. But the Argentine defense seemed too strong. Back and forth, back and forth, at breakneck speed they went, and finally Pelé saw his chance. One of his teammates passed him the ball. Pelé handled it deftly, and as he watched the same teammate position himself downfield, he realized he had a chance to set up a goal. With a well-placed kick, Pelé passed the ball back, and his teammate kicked it into the goal.

The stadium exploded! The rest of the Brazilian team mobbed their two teammates who had been responsible for the goal. Happy and proud, Pelé thought of his family and friends back in Bauru. He knew they were listening to the game on the radio, and he knew they were happy and proud, too. His mother and grandmother would surely understand now why he just had to go to São Paulo.

Unfortunately, the next goal was scored by the Argentines, and they won the game. The next game, however, the Brazilians won, and they went on to win the Rocca Cup. The last game was held at Pacaembu Stadium in São Paulo. By that time Pelé was no longer on the reserve team but on the starting team. He scored the first goal, and when the Brazilians won that game, and the Cup, there was no question that the youngster from Bauru had established himself. If there had been an MVP (Most Valuable Player) award for the tournament, he surely would have won it. As it was, he was named Athlete of the Year in Brazilian soccer, for even though he was only seventeen, he had scored more goals than any other Brazilian player that season.

Shortly thereafter, Pelé suffered his first serious injury. In a game against another Brazilian team, he received a kick on the knee from an opposing player who was trying to get the ball away from him. Instantly, Pelé fell down and rolled on the grass in pain. He was surrounded by his teammates and coaches and carried off the field on a stretcher. In his pain, all Pelé could think of was his father. Would this knee injury hamper his career? Would he prove unable to fulfill his father's dream?

His teammates assured him he would be all right. The team doctor did the same. The team masseur promised that he would take care of Pelé's injured knee and that Pelé would soon be in good shape again. Pelé tried to believe them, but he was so frightened that he feared the worst. "I didn't know how to feel about the guy who did it," Pelé says. "I heard all kinds of comments about it. One would say he did it purposely, and others would say it was an accident. But I knew how responsible he was for that and for my future games."[9]

The games that loomed in Pelé's immediate future were those of the 1958 World Cup Tournament. Each team selected its best players, and it was from these selected players that the final Brazilian World Cup team would be chosen, a few from each major team. Despite his injured knee, Pelé was one of the initial selections.

After all the players were selected, they began an endless round of workouts, checkups, exercises, and training periods. As a boy in the streets of Bauru, Pelé had played soccer for hours on end, but these workouts in preparation for the World Cup were like nothing he had ever experienced before. And, of course, after all that work, there was no guarantee that he would be one of the final choices. In many ways it was, as Pelé recalls, "a nightmare."

At last there was a meeting with the coaches and directors—a meeting at which the final list of chosen athletes was named. Pelé was relieved that his name was on the list. But at the same time he was saddened, for some of his friends' names were not. He knew how they, and their parents, must feel, and he thought himself very, very lucky.

The team of chosen players took off shortly on a

"warm-up" trip to play against other Brazilian teams. Pelé visited his family in Bauru first, and while they were happy and excited for him, they were also worried about his injury. He assured them that he felt fine. But privately, Pelé was worried, too. He had not fully recuperated.

On the advice of the team doctor, Pelé took it easy during the warm-up trip, playing only until his knee began to pain him. He spent hours doing exercises and having his knee massaged. He concentrated on getting well, he willed the pain to go away. But as the time approached for the team to leave Brazil and go to Sweden, his knee still did not feel completely right.

Before the trip to Europe, the Brazilian National Team visited the President of Brazil, Suscelino Kubitscheck. One by one they were introduced to him by the team director. He already knew most by sight, for he was as big a soccer fan as anyone else in Brazil, and he knew several of the players' names. For each, he had an encouraging word or a little joke. Then it was Pelé's turn.

"And this is Pelé, Mr. President," the team director said. "The youngest of the team, he is only seventeen."

"I see this is the new Brazil," the President said. "I am very happy to meet you, Pelé."[10]

The new Brazil—Pelé repeated that phrase over and over to himself. Could he indeed live up to that prediction? If only he had not suffered that injury to his knee. He determined that it would get better. More than anything else, he wanted to be the new Brazil.

When the team left Brazil for Sweden, a huge crowd of reporters and well-wishers gathered at the airport to see them off. They called out to the older, better-known members of the team—Hey Bellini! Hey Vava! It seemed to Pelé that everyone had someone to say good-bye, a relative or a friend—everyone but him. He understood that his parents could not travel all that way just to see him off, but he felt very small and very lonely as he mounted the steps to the plane. Then suddenly he heard his name.

"Pelé! Pelé!"

He turned to see who could possibly know him. There in the crowd was a youth about his age, waving to him. It was just a young person who knew who he was and wanted to wish him well. Smiling and no longer depressed at all, Pelé waved back and then happily entered the plane.

For Pelé, the trip to Sweden was an exciting one. He had dreamed of one day being a great soccer player and traveling all over the world, but he had never really imagined himself flying on an airplane over the wide blue ocean or riding through the green countryside of Sweden. He marveled at the blond, blue-eyed people and their customs and tried hard to remember everything so he could tell his parents when he returned home. The entire country, it seemed, was excited about the World Cup Tournament to which it was playing host. Sweden had an excellent team that year. No one, however, was more excited than Pelé. He would see the most famous soccer players in the world and perhaps play in the tournament that every young soccer player dreams about.

Before the actual start of the tournament there were a few days of scrimmaging and working out so the teams that had traveled from distant places would be ready for the games. Sometimes Pelé's knee would swell up and hurt, and he was terribly afraid he would be unable to play. Several times he went to the coach and the director of the team and asked to be sent back to Brazil and replaced on the team by another player. Though he wanted more than anything else to play in the World Cup tournament, he thought first of his team, and he did not want to do anything to hamper its chances.

The coach and director refused even to consider his request. He was an excellent player, though young, and they were confident that he would be able to play despite his injured knee. They did realize, however, that his low spirits were more of a problem than his injury. They sent him to the team psychiatrist, who told him to stop worrying and to be more of a man about it. This really hurt Pelé. It is disturbing to any youth to be accused of not being manly, but it is particularly troublesome for a Latin American boy. He could not explain that deep down inside he was terrified that the same thing that had happened to his father would happen to him, that his knee injury would prevent him from rising to the top in soccer. He felt his fear was real and justified and that he was being unjustly accused of acting like a child. But the psychiatrist's words did cause him to snap out of his depression. He determined to put his fears in the back of his mind and to play better than he had ever played before.

Pelé was so "up" for his team's first game, against Austria, that he nearly cried when he learned he was only on the reserve team. But then he looked at his other teammates who were listed on the reserve team and realized he was being foolish. They were in perfect shape and yet were not on the starting team. He was recovering from an injury. They did not appear to be unhappy, so why should he be?

On the day of the game, Pelé and the other players on the reserve team joined the Brazilian delegation in the stadium to cheer their team. After a difficult beginning, Brazil made a goal, then another, then another. They beat Austria to win their first round of the World Cup Tournament, and in Brazil's locker room there was joyous celebration. Pelé had gone to the locker room when the game was over, and nearly every starting-team player took the time to say something to cheer him up. "You'll soon be okay," they said. "Don't worry." Pelé realized how lucky he was to have such caring teammates and was very grateful.

The second game was against England, and this time Pelé felt ready. His knee, though not yet completely healed, was not bothering him much, and he was impatient to see action. But once again his name was not on the list of starters. He began to wonder if he had traveled all the way to Sweden and World Cup competition just to sit in the stadium and cheer like an average fan.

The English were a tough team, and they played very well, but Brazil, at least in the opinion of its team and fans, was better. Still, while Brazil managed to prevent England from scoring, England's strong defense kept Brazil from scoring. When the score remained at 0–0 at half time, there was visible anxiety on the faces of the entire Brazilian delegation. As the second half progressed, the anxiety increased, and when the game ended with a 0–0 score, there was great despair. The coach, however, reminded his players that at least they had not lost; their time would come, he assured them, and it was their job to get ready for it.

The next game was against the Soviet Union, and to his great joy Pelé's name was announced among those of the other starters. In a flash, it seemed, he was standing with his teammates facing a line of Soviet players as the national anthems were played. "I felt pride, and my thoughts went back to Brazil," says Pelé. "I could imagine my whole family listening to the radio, not only them, but also my friends and my whole country. I felt great and forgot completely about my knee. I was going to defend Brazil and do it well."[11]

But during this, his very first World Cup game, Pelé was nervous. The Soviet goalkeeper looked huge, and it seemed to Pelé that the man could easily cover the entire goal with his body. Pelé missed two good chances to send the ball whizzing into the Soviet goal, and he did not get a third chance. Brazil won the game, 1–0, and though he did not score, Pelé played well enough to remain on the starting team for the next game, the quarterfinals against France.

The game opened rather unexpectedly. France scored a goal within minutes, and Pelé was so taken by surprise that, forgetting that his team had a goalkeeper to do such things, he ran into his own net, retrieved the ball, and personally ran it right up to the kickoff circle. Then he, the youngest member of the team, gathered the other Brazilian players around him and delivered a pep talk! To this day, he cannot remember what he said, but the incident reveals how confident he was; and whatever he said, it may have helped his team. His actions certainly did. He went on to score three goals!

That was the roughest game he had ever played in. The French deliberately used violent tactics. Pelé was hit twice on his injured knee, and each time the pain was so sharp that he was not sure he could go on. By that time, the entire stadium, practically, was against France because of the team's rough play, and the Brazilians were cheered with every move they made. Brazil won the game 5–2, and it was an especially sweet triumph, for they had refused to lower themselves by being violent in return.

Brazil won the semifinals against Wales 1–0, and it was Pelé who made that single goal of the game. It was a spectacular play. Pelé, his back to the opponents' net, lobbed a kick over his head against the body of one of the Welsh players, wheeled around, and booted home the goal before the ball could touch the ground!

By this time he had become a favorite among the spectators at the tournament, partly because of his youth (he was the youngest player in the tournament), partly because of his excellent play, and partly, too, because he was black. "At that point I was very popular, especially with the kids," Pelé recalls. "They were amazed by my color. They would come to me, touch my black skin, and then rub their hands on their faces, thinking that I was painted black and that the paint would color their skin. It was very funny and they were beautiful kids."[12] Adult fans recognized him, too, and wherever he went he attracted a crowd. Seeing this, his friends cautioned him not to let all the attention go to his head, but Pelé saw no reason why it should. Certainly he was popular, but he was still the same person.

At last the day arrived for the final game of the tournament. Whoever won the game would win the World Cup, and it would either be Brazil or Sweden. Brazil was favored, but the Swedish team was playing in its own country, and the crowd would definitely favor the home team. Crowd reaction is as important in soccer as in any other sport, and the Brazilian players were very aware of the effect of the crowd. Besides, the Swedish team was also very good.

"When we were lined up for the match ready to start the game, I thought about my father," says Pelé. "How was he feeling? Was he proud of me? Of course he would be. I was glad I was giving them some happiness, just thinking about the hard times I gave them as a kid; but those days were gone and everything was fine."[13]

As play began, the predominantly Swedish crowd set up a chant in support of its team, and, as if in answer, within five minutes the Swedes had made a goal. Pelé could hardly believe, it had come so suddenly; he tried not to panic. Watching the reaction of the Brazilians, the coach of the Swedish team hoped that they would indeed panic. Unfortunately, Brazilian National Teams in the past had been undone for this reason. They had worried about being behind so early in the game and, in their attempts to catch up, had made costly mistakes.

This time, however, the Brazilians did not panic.

Garrincha (which means Little Bird) began to lead his team's offense. He was a very fast runner, and he began to move the ball down the field at a furious pace every time he got it. On one such run he suddenly began to move even faster, and in a flash he crossed the ball to his teammate Vava, who smashed it into the goal. The score was now 1–1.

Garrincha continued his furious pace, and now Pelé joined him in maintaining it. One of Pelé's shots curled against a Swedish post and ricocheted out. Then he fed the ball to "Cobra" Didi in the midfield, who passed it to Garrincha, who passed it to Vava. Vava found the net. The score was 2–1.

The stadium was practically silent now, the chanting had stopped. The crowd and the Swedish team alike seemed hypnotized by the precise, rhythmic stroking of the ball from player to player and the sudden acceleration toward the goal. It was a fantastic display of individual player talents within the over-all structure of great team play.

Ten minutes into the second half, Pelé, while remaining part of the team, began to emerge as the star of the game. Receiving a pass from a teammate, he played a little game with the ball with the instep of his foot. Then, suddenly, he flicked the ball over the Swedish goalkeeper. The crowd could hardly believe its eyes.

Sweden scored a second goal, but Zagalo scored a

fourth for Brazil. The game was nearly over, and the Brazilian team was so excited that they fairly skipped along the field, wide grins on their faces. It was hardly a time when they would be expected to score another goal. Then Zagalo made a high pass to Pelé, whose back was to the net. He caught the ball on his thigh, turned, and with one swift, smooth motion, headed it into the net. The game ended and Pelé, crying with joy, fell into the arms of his teammates.

King Gustav of Sweden presented the World Cup to Bellini, the captain of the Brazilian team, and then personally congratulated the rest of the team. Then he left the field, and Pelé and his teammates ran two laps of honor around it while the audience cheered and applauded a fine team for a fine performance. When they tried to leave the stadium, they were prevented from doing so by a crowd of reporters, photographers, and autograph-seekers. A delegation of Soviet reporters presented Pelé with a cup for being the youngest athlete of the championship tournament.

Back in the locker room at last, the order was to celebrate, to forget about the routine, getting enough sleep, even not drinking. Anything goes! the coach cried. After all those months of preparation, exercises, and tension, they were soccer champions of the world!

Little did they know, at the time, that their victory was the beginning of Brazilian dominance of world soccer for many years to come.

5 From "Idol Kid" to Big Crocodile

The return trip was the longest the team had ever experienced. At every stop the plane made, they were greeted by the press and well-wishers, special ceremonies and celebrations. Naturally, Pelé and his teammates accepted these honors graciously, but they were tired and spent, and they wanted to get home. They had no idea what awaited them in Brazil.

When the plane finally landed at the airport in Recife, it seemed to the members of the team that the entire city was waiting for them. It was raining, but that had not kept away the huge crowd of people who wanted to see and congratulate their national heroes. Pelé watched as his teammate Vava was met at the bottom of the plane's steps and carried to the terminal by a joyous group of well-wishers. He was pleased for his teammate, for Vava was a truly great player, and a star. Little did Pelé suspect that exactly the same thing was about to happen to him. Reaching the bottom of the steps, he was mobbed by the crowd, and hoisted aloft for the bumpiest and happiest trip between plane and terminal that he had ever experienced. Everywhere he looked, adoring eyes were turned to him. They called him "Idol Kid."

A similar reception awaited them in São Paulo and at the other Brazilian airports where the plane stopped. The entire country was celebrating, and it was only proper for the team to recognize the tribute their countrymen were paying them. The exhausted team moved as if hypnotized through crowd after crowd, their eyes vacant, their smiles fixed on their faces, their hands smarting from too many handshakes. They were honored by the attention they received, but they wished they could get just a little rest. By the time they reached Rio de Janeiro, however, they had perked up. "In Rio we met our families," Pelé later explained, "and I'll never forget when I saw my parents—my mother and father were crying, and I was crying, everybody was crying."

But then it was on to more public celebration. "Celebrations, parties, prizes happened all over, day after day," Pelé recalls. "In Rio there was a carnival in the streets, the whole country was going mad over the victory. During the rides in the streets we sometimes would starve to death. We had no time for anything. Sometimes we had to ask for something [to eat]; otherwise we would have fainted. No one would leave us alone. It was incredible."[1]

They were given cars and considerable sums of money. The President received the team at his palace and presented them with special medals. Every night they had to remove flowers and confetti from their hair and clothes and massage their cheeks, sore from so much smiling. At last, the team members were permitted to separate and to return to their respective hometowns. But there again, celebrations awaited them.

Arriving in Bauru, Pelé was greeted by signs that read: WELCOME HOME PELÉ, SON OF BAURU AND CHAMPION OF THE WORLD. The mayor was waiting with official congratulations, and in the days that followed Pelé would be the honored guest at a variety of celebrations. All he wanted to do was to go home, talk with his family, enjoy one of his mother's meals, and go to bed and sleep for as long as it took to feel rested again; but it was days before he was able to do so. Pelé was learning that being a star involved a great deal of responsibility to one's fans. It meant smiling and shaking hands when all he really wanted to do was be alone. It meant answering reporters' questions when he was almost too tired to speak. Basically, it meant understanding that the fans, in their enthusiasm, forgot that he was a human being who needed to eat and sleep and have privacy just like everyone else. His youngster's dreams had not included these aspects of fame, and it was all very new to Pelé.

Shortly after his return, he was informed that he was in for yet another new experience—the Army. In the United States, it was often possible for a young star athlete to avoid the Army. Not so in Brazil. Pelé was of age; therefore he had to join the Army and serve one compulsory year. Fortunately, he was a peacetime soldier, and thus he was able to continue to play for the Santos club. However, he also had to play for the Army team and the National Team. Once he found himself playing seven games in fourteen days—a remarkable feat, considering that he usually lost between four and six pounds per game. All these games, however, did cause him to amass an impressive number of goals in that year, 1959: 118, compared to 40 in 1957 and 73 in 1958. Meanwhile, he had to attend to all his other soldierly duties, which, for Pelé, were harder than they were for the average soldier.

"It was very exhausting because nobody would realize that I was just like everybody else," Pelé recalls ruefully. "I couldn't be tired, I was a champion and they were all expecting too much from me. In the Army my commanders would make me do things like sweeping floors, cleaning offices, just to make sure I was just like the other recruits and not a star. It was tough but I had my duty and I was going to go through it just like the other soldiers."[2]

Pelé survived the Army and returned to the Santos club full-time, having completed his required service to his country. With his team, he traveled across Latin America, playing other teams, winning every match. His money, always turned over to his father and invested wisely by the older man, grew and grew. Then, in 1960, when Pelé was twenty, he asked for and received the tremendous salary of $150,000 per year, a $27,000 cash bonus, and a new Volkswagen. In the same year, he did something he had always dreamed of doing: He bought a home for his family. His mother chose it and decorated it. It was a large, comfortable house in one of the better sections of Bauru. Pelé felt prouder about it than about anything he had ever done before. And, needless to say, his mother stopped complaining about the obsession with soccer that seemed to afflict the males of her family. Still, she refused to attend any of the games in which Pelé played. The only games she would watch were televised games aired after the actual games were played, for these she could watch knowing her son had come through them without injury.

By now, Pelé was one of the foremost soccer stars in Brazil, and he was fast becoming one of the most popular soccer idols in other countries as well. There were some foreign teams that wanted him enough to offer him big money to leave Brazil. The first offer came in 1959, to go to Paris. Pelé was making very little money at the time, and the offer was so good that many of his teammates urged him to accept it. In 1960, the Spanish team, Real Madrid, also made an excellent offer. But Pelé accepted neither. He did not want to play soccer just for money; he wanted to play for a team he liked in an area he liked. Besides, he did not want to be so far away from his family. The people in other countries would have to be content to see Pelé when his team played exhibition games in their countries.

In 1960, during a Santos exhibition tour in Mexico, Pelé was injured in the left shoulder in a match against an Argentinian team in Mexico City. Thus he intended to stay out of the next game, in Guadalajara, Mexico. But the fans in Guadalajara wanted to see Pelé play, and they would not stop shouting his name. Not wishing to disappoint the fans, the nineteen-year-old entered the game in the second half. His shoulder hurt a bit, but he hardly felt it in his joy at being wanted so by the fans. In fact, he was so happy he could hardly control himself. Every time he or a teammate made a goal or a particularly fine play, he would leap up and punch the air with his right fist. That "jump of victory," as it later came to be called, would become a trademark of Pelé's and famous throughout the world.

Soon, back in Brazil, the nickname "Idol Kid" had been replaced by "Perola Negro," or Black Pearl. Pelé did not mind being called this or any other nickname, but he wished sometimes that people would just call him by his real name, Edson. For most observers, however, Pelé just had to be spoken about in superlatives. He continued to score an amazing number of goals—74 in 1960—but often it was not the goals themselves that were so incredible as the way he made them. The lightning-fast moves and deft passes, the accurateness of his "heading," the control he possessed in his legs and feet, all combining in a seemingly magical sequence that more often than not resulted in a goal. So remarkable were his physical abilities that a major university once asked if he would be willing to une tests so medical experts could find out t was that made Pelé "tick." Amiably, he

For weeks he went to the university laboratory where experts prodded him, wired his head for readings, and measured his muscles. They came up with some interesting results. When he was in training, his heart, they found, beat about 56–58 times per minute. The heart of the average athlete in training beats 90–95 times per minute. The average athlete must rest several minutes after performing some feat before he can repeat it. Pelé could repeat a great effort within 45–60 seconds. His "peripheral vision," the ability to see on both sides while looking straight ahead, was found to be 30 per cent greater than that of the average athlete. The bone in his heel was found to be exceptionally strong and well developed, so that when he ran he was forced to bend forward. This helped to explain his great speed. The same bone acted as a kind of shock absorber after a jump or a high kick.

Pelé could run 100 meters in 11 seconds and jump almost 6 feet high. He jumped earlier than other players to head the ball because he had the ability to hover longer in the air. With each new measurement the university medical experts were more amazed. Concluding all their tests, they announced that he would have been a genius in whatever physical endeavor he had chosen.

Pelé was then, and continues to be, very modest about his physical ability, calling it a gift from God. "I feel the divine gift to make something out of nothing," he says. "You need balance and speed of mind and strength. But there is something else that God has given me. It's an extra instinct I have for the game. Sometimes I can take the ball and no one can foresee any danger. And then, two or three seconds later, there is a goal. This doesn't make me proud, it makes me humble because it is a talent that God gave me."[3]

This "extra instinct" of Pelé's may have been a God-given one, but Pelé nevertheless worked hard to develop it. He spent hour upon grueling hour training, day after day. Rarely did he have a day off, for to do so would have been to make practically worthless his training during previous days. He pushed his body to the limits of its endurance, then pushed it more. He also trained his mind. The man who, as a youngster, had disliked school and played hookey as often as possible began a study of the history of soccer. He also took lessons in geometry and learned to play chess in order to perfect his game. Actually, sometimes out on the soccer fields it did appear that he was playing as if on a giant chess board. He seemed to know what his opponents would do five or ten moves ahead of time. There was the game he played for Santos in 1961, for example, in which he took a pass in his own team's half of the field, dribbled downfield past *seven* opponents, eluded the goalkeeper, and scored! The opposing team was a talented one; it's just that Pelé read their moves before they made them! His concentration was excellent. The medical experts who tested him, by the way, also did mental tests, and concluded that he would have been a genius in any *mental* endeavor he chose as well.

Pelé's chief mental endeavor, in his early twenties, was the game of soccer. But he intended to put his mind to other matters in the future. He knew that he would not be able to play professional soccer for an indefinite number of years. In fact, when he was about twenty, he expected that he would only play professionally until 1965, when he would be twenty-five. At that point, he figured, he would have reached his soccer-playing peak. After that, he would still continue to play soccer, but on an amateur basis, when and where he wanted. He would participate in championships to defend his country and Brazil's name, but he would not belong to any club or organization.

There was another reason why Pelé only wanted to play professional soccer until 1965. He figured that twenty-five or so would be a good age at which to get married, and he did not think marriage and a career in professional soccer worked very well together. He saw how difficult the situation sometimes was for his married teammates, who were forced to be away from home for long periods of time, often leaving sick children or unhappy wives. He did not want that for himself.

So, continuing to take advice from his father, Pelé lived quite simply, invested his money wisely, and played soccer.

In 1962, Brazil was invited once again to participate in the World Cup Tournament, hosted that year by Chile. This time, of course, Pelé was named to the starting team immediately, and what's more, he was in perfect shape, unplagued by injuries. He was experiencing an excellent phase with regard to his playing, and was scoring a lot of goals. This World Cup competition was much more "tranquil" for the entire Brazilian National Team. Most of the players were World Cup veterans, having played in the 1958 tournament, and thus the team was very mature and very "together." Brazil advanced easily through the complex elimination matches until they met Czechoslovakia. In that game, Pelé suffered a serious bruise of the knee and was forced to leave the field. He realized how grave the situation was for his team, for he had little time to recuperate before the final phase of the tournament; and he took pains to give support to his substitute, who played excellently in his place for the next few games. By the time of the final game, against Mexico, to decide the winner of the World Cup, Pelé's knee was much better, and in his opinion he could play almost as well as he had before the injury. In the opinion of the game's observers, he was as good as ever. During that game, he made one of the more spectacular plays of his career.

Putting on a sudden burst of speed, he scooted half the length of the field, reversed himself, and outsmarted two opposing players to loft the ball into the upper corner of the net. Brazil won the game, 2–1, and had its second consecutive World Cup victory, to become only the second country to win two tournaments in a row. (Italy had won the Cup in 1934 and 1938). Pelé gave a big kick and leaped to embrace his teammates. Then, suddenly, he became very frightened. He thought about his bruise, about how, a few days before, he had not even been able to walk. He had been so worried about how his injury would affect his team and their chances in the tournament, so concerned about their progress, that only now did he realize how seriously injured he had been, how close he had come to the end of his career.

Back in Brazil, celebration was wild—equally as joyous as it had been in 1958—and Pelé's national stature rose to even greater heights. What other athlete has been the subject of a national law? After it was rumored that Italy was trying to interest Pelé in going to that country to play soccer, the Brazilian Government considered Pelé so vital to the country's reputation that it passed a law forbidding him to be traded out of the country! In a way, Pelé had become a national resource.

Practically anywhere he went, he was recognized and mobbed. He was besieged by interview requests, offered big money in exchange for his endorsement of all kinds of commercial products, and hounded by autograph seekers. And yet, though he freely admitted his talent, calling it a gift from God, he remained humble about his superstardom.

Once, around 1964, the Santos team rented five taxicabs to take them to a motel where they would stay before playing a road game. Four hours later, four of the cabs arrived at their destination, but the one carrying Pelé and two of his teammates was missing. Perhaps, the rest of the team thought, they had stopped along the way to eat or to rest. But hours passed, and still no fifth taxicab. By this time, the coach and the rest of the team were very worried, and they were relieved when at last a private car arrived with the three players inside. Their taxi had broken down, and it had taken them all that time to find a car to transport them.

The rest of the team couldn't understand why the three hadn't simply flagged down a passing car on the highway. Surely any motorist would be happy to give the famous Pelé a lift.

Pelé answered, "Can you imagine three black boys hitching at night? Do you think somebody would stop?"[4]

As a matter of fact, he was right. Pelé and his teammates had asked people for a lift at corners and lights, but it had been dark and people were suspicious. It was hours before one man they flagged down had agreed to take them.

As had happened often in the past, Pelé had forgotten to use his name.

Many U.S. sports stars would have publicized such an incident, using it to point out the racism in the United States that afflicts them. Stars like Kareem Abdul-Jabbar and Bill Russell in basketball, Muhammad Ali in boxing, and Henry Aaron in baseball have waited until they reached stardom and then used their position to try to educate the white public regarding the burden the black person, even a black sports superstar, must carry in the United

States. Pelé, being not just a national but an international star, could have done the same thing but on a worldwide scale. Some observers regard his not doing so as a failure, a missed opportunity. Others are pleased he did not, being mindful of the publicity it would have caused. As for Pelé himself, he was not much concerned with such opinions. He insisted he personally had not experienced racial discrimination, either in Brazil or elsewhere. In Brazil, he explained whenever he was asked about it, the problems of color were more social than racial. And in other countries he could recall no racial slurs having been aimed at him. There have been a few racial incidents in which he has been involved and in which he has taken a stand. One such incident occurred in Dakar, Senegal. Having learned which hotel Pelé was staying in, a crowd of black residents of Dakar formed outside, hoping to catch a glimpse of him. The French proprietess of the hotel called them "savages." When the Dakar police heard this, they arrested the woman. As the incident had occurred in a way because of Pelé, friends of the woman asked that he intercede on her behalf. However, the usually accommodating Pelé refused. In calling them "savages," he explained, the woman had offended the people who were waiting for him, people of his color, and thus he felt offended. The woman remained in jail until Pelé left Dakar.

Pelé's feeling is that sports is one thing and that politics and religion are quite another, and that the two should not be combined. He is aware that there are people who desire to use him for their own ends, and he tries very hard to avoid getting into such situations. Yet he has nothing negative to say about those blacks who do speak out against racism. For example, he says he respects Muhammad Ali and that Ali had a very different childhood and very different experiences from his own and thus naturally has different racial attitudes than he himself has.

Pelé will not endorse political candidates or attend any function that has too many political overtones. "If a Prime Minister or a King wishes to meet me," says Pelé, "I gladly go to the palace for lunch or some talk. But I do not mix with politics or religion. I am Brazilian, but I feel everywhere at home."

Pelé's personal trainer, Julio Mazzei, supports this notion of Pelé's: "When Pelé is in Spain, the people there believe he is Spanish. When he is in England, they feel he is English. Russia, Yugoslavia, Turkey, France, it is all the same. . . ."[5]

There is no doubt that one reason why he is so

universally popular is that he has stayed away from religion and politics, but his phenomenal popularity is based on much more. No one, however, can define exactly what it is that helps him transcend the barriers of race, religion, and politics around the world.

In 1970, during the height of the Biafran war in Nigeria, both sides agreed to cease fighting if he would play two exhibition games. He played the first game in Nigeria. The next day a Nigerian Army captain escorted him halfway across the river separating the two sides, and turned him over to a Biafran Army captain. Pelé played a second game for the Biafran side. The next day, Pelé left and the war resumed.

This was not the only time a cease-fire was called on his behalf. Political disputes in Khartoum and Algeria have also been interrupted in his honor.

At least one foreign President has interceded in a game on behalf of Pelé's team. The incident occurred in January of 1969 in Brazzaville, Congo (now Zaïre). The Santos team had come to play an exhibition game, and the President, who led the opening ceremonies, personally shook hands with each member of the team. However, the Congolese team did not share their President's sense of courtesy toward the visitors. From the very beginning of the match, the Santos players, particularly Pelé, were hit and kicked violently; yet the referee refused to call a foul against the Congolese team. Under such circumstances, Santos announced that they neither would nor could continue the game. The President then sent a note to the referee suggesting that if he did not call the fouls, did not conduct the game properly, he would be arrested. Santos was there, the President reminded the referee, to give a show, and *he,* the President, wanted to see that show. The match began again, and almost immediately the referee called a foul against the Congo team. From then on, the game was judged properly. Santos won, 3–2, and everyone was pleased with the game.

Once, in Hong Kong, Pelé and some friends went to the border between that Crown Colony and Communist China. Recognizing him, two Red Chinese border guards put down their machine guns and crossed the buffer zone to shake his hand. They could have been shot for doing so, but obviously both the other Communist Chinese guards and the Hong Kong guards understood their desire to meet Pelé.

By the time Pelé was in his early twenties, invitations had come to him for visits to just about every court and presidential palace on five continents, and nearly everywhere people had a pet name for him.

In France he was "La Tulipe Noire" (The Black Tulip); in Chile "El Peligro" (The Dangerous One); in Italy "Il Re" (The King). Whatever the names, all expressed the magic of Pelé.

Certainly, part of his magic was his phenomenal soccer talent, and part was his care not to criticize others, his feeling for the other fellow. Nowhere was this characteristic more evident than in Dakar, Senegal, on May 28, 1967. The Santos team arrived there, after a tour through Europe and the Americas, for its first game in Africa, against the National Team of Senegal. During the first half of the game, teammate Zito made a pass to Pelé, who quietly and easily dribbled past the Senegalese defenders and goalkeeper and scored. The goal came as a complete surprise to the Senegalese goalkeeper and, angry at himself and highly embarrassed, the man kicked the goalpost, burst into tears, and left the field.

Seeing the goalkeeper's consternation and understanding his embarrassment, Pelé followed the man off the field and apologized for making the goal. However, the goalkeeper could not be comforted. The Santos players didn't know what to do. Before the second half began, Pelé had an idea. He suggested to his teammates that they not play as hard and try not to score too many goals. In this way, the other team would not feel so embarrassed. The match ended with the score 4–1 in Santos' favor. The people of Dakar were pleased that Santos had only scored four goals against their team, and Pelé and his teammates were pleased that they had not unduly embarrassed their opponents.

Still another reason behind Pelé's appeal was his modesty and simplicity. Right in the middle of an interview with reporters, he thought nothing of bending down to tie a child's shoelace.

But Pelé was no pushover, except perhaps when it came to kids. Once in London, for example, he paused during a stroll with Prince Philip to talk with English schoolchildren. He had shown he was his own man in many ways, among them, in his refusal to be used as a political pawn. He had also developed a very strong survival instinct when it came to dealing with his fame. His excellent peripheral vision was useful not only on the soccer field but also in crowds. All the while he was answering reporters' questions or signing autographs, his eyes were alert for escape routes should the crowd become unruly.

The waiting room of the office from which he conducted his various businesses was always filled with reporters. Thus Pelé had a secret way to get to his office without being seen. He would get off the elevator on the floor below, go along a special corridor, and enter his office through a door that could not be seen from the waiting room. Out of necessity, his best friends and advisers became unofficial bodyguards, and Pelé, whose one fear outside of knee injuries is kidnaping, welcomed their presence. Traveling about was a major problem, and in a way it is surprising that Pelé, who could afford it, never bought his own plane. Wherever he went he was forced to move in secrecy, and press teletype reports were often coded to protect his privacy. An example from June 1974: "THE BIG CROCODILE WILL GO TO FRANKFURT." Only a few high officials would know that the Big Crocodile was Pelé.

6 Pelé Settles Down

Pelé got married in 1966, and it came as a great surprise to everyone but his closest friends. Somehow this most famous athlete in the world had managed to court his new bride secretly for *six years!*

Her name was Rosemarie de Cholby, and she was a native of Santos, where her father worked for the harbor authority. Pelé first saw her on a rainy day in 1960 when he and a group of Santos players stopped in at a local gymnasium and became interested in a girls' basketball game that was in progress. In truth, they were probably less interested in the game than in the girls themselves, especially one pretty young girl on the bench. Pelé and his friends wanted to see her play, and from the stands they called out to the coach, urging that the girl be put into the game. Despite their protests, the coach would not put the girl in.

Meanwhile, Pelé was attracted by the girl and wanted to get to know her better. He managed to find out that she worked in a record shop, and he began to stop by, at first under the pretense of buying a record, and later just to talk. Pelé could have had many women. Wherever he went, he was surrounded by them, and any of them would gladly have become his girl. But he was rather shy, and not the sort to take advantage of his fame where women were concerned. Then, too, he realized that many were attracted to his fame and to his money rather than to him as a person. He did want to get married some day, he would tell reporters, "But I think it is going to be difficult to choose the right one because I want a woman who will like me as a person, who can understand me as a human being, not a soccer star."[1] He had had very few dates in his lifetime, and up until the time he met Rosemarie had never really been in love. But as the weeks passed, and he became a more frequent visitor to the record shop, gradually he realized he was falling in love with Rosemarie.

He did not, however, make his romance public. He was only twenty years old, and he did not wish to rush into marriage; he wanted to be sure. Also, he was against mixing soccer and marriage, having seen the pressures it placed on his teammates. As the years passed, he became sure that Rosie, as he liked to call her, was the woman he wanted for his wife. And he became less set against combining marriage with his soccer-playing career. But he and Rosie continued to wait and to see each other in secret, for as Pelé became more and more famous, anyone related to him became an increasingly greater public attraction and a more likely victim of kidnaping. Pelé feared that Rosie's life would be disrupted by the publicity and that she could be placed in danger of kidnaping if their relationship were made public. For her part, Rosemarie understood. She was a very sensitive and mature young woman, and Pelé's peace of mind was far more important to her than public recognition of their love for each other. In her, he had indeed found a woman who was interested in him as a person and not in his money and fame.

And so, for six years, they courted in secret. They rarely went out in public together, for there was too much risk that Pelé would be recognized. So careful were they that Rosie never even attended a game in which Pelé played. When at long last they were married, it was in a small, private ceremony in Pelé's home.

At first, public reaction was one of shock. Pelé married! The Brazilian people had become so accus-

On June 10, 1975, the day he arrived in the United States, Pelé attended a New York Cosmos game. While he did not play in the match between the Cosmos and the Philadelphia Atoms, he took part in the pregame ceremonies and kicked an autographed ball into the stands at Veterans Stadium in Philadelphia. *(Wide World Photos)*

Using his famous deft footwork, P
takes the ball downfield through
forest of opponents in a game betw
the Cosmos and the San Jose Ear
quakes. *(United Press Internatio
Photo)*

With a truly "heads up" play, Pelé heads the ball toward the goal as a Boston Minutemen player tries to kick it away. The play occurred during the first half of the game at Downing Stadium. Soccer experts agree that no one can head the ball as expertly as Pelé can. *(Wide World Photos)*

The Venezuelan goalkeeper could only watch helplessly from the ground as Pelé kicked in the sixth goal for his Santos team in a game in Rio de Janeiro. Pelé's amazing ability to hover in midair makes it possible for him to take more time to aim before taking his shot. *(Wide World Photos)*

Pelé displays some of his fancy footwork during a game between the Cosmos and the Washington (D.C.) Diplomats. The game, which the Cosmos won, 9–2, drew a record soccer crowd of 35,620 fans to Robert F. Kennedy Stadium. *(United Press International Photo)*

Pelé's exciting career has included much more than soccer. He is a successful businessman, and has tried his hand at acting as well. In 1971 he played the starring role in a Brazilian film about Chico Bondade, a free Black who led a slave revolt in Brazil in the 1880s. *(United Press International Photo)*

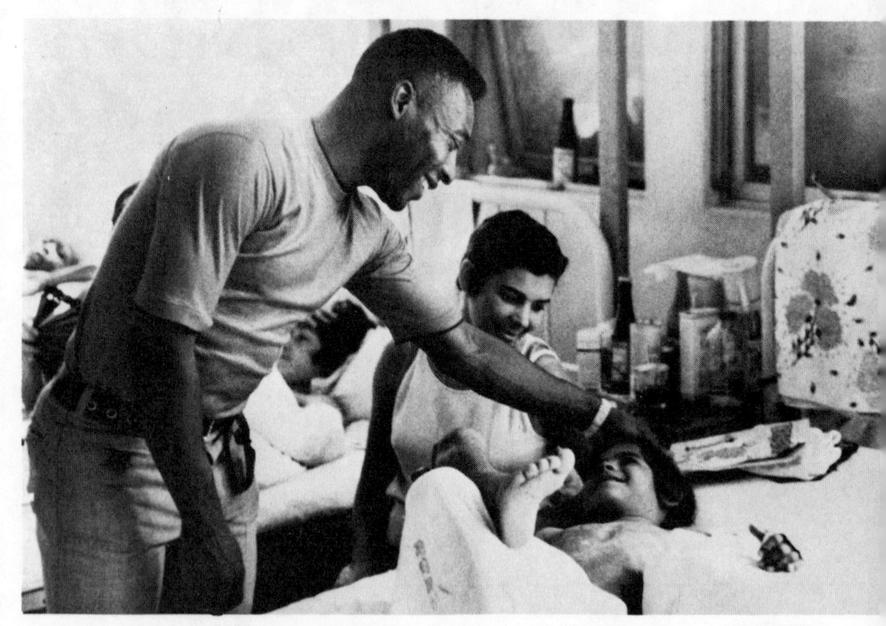

At the Brazilian hospital where he used to receive his medical checkups before beginning training, Pelé would visit small patients. Unlike many other sports superstars, he takes time to sign autographs and is never too busy to brighten a child's day with a few kind words. *(United Press International Photo)*

tomed to the bachelorhood of their No. 1 star that it was hard to imagine him any other way. There was recognition of the fact that Pelé was black and Rosemarie was white, but the couple did not experience any adverse publicity about it. Perhaps one reason was that Pelé was so famous and popular in Brazil, but whatever the reason, the couple never experienced any racial problems. The story was big news for a few months, but gradually the majority of the Brazilian people came to accept Pelé's marriage.

The marriage would prove to be a stable and lasting one. The couple continued to avoid going out in public, for Pelé would always be mobbed by fans who recognized him. Rosemarie was fiercely protective of their private life and made their home a haven for her husband. They wasted no time in starting a family. In 1967 their daughter, Kelly Christina, was born. Pelé's family became the most important thing in his life and the source of his greatest happiness. He decided that, for a few years more at least, he could combine a soccer career and family life. He often commented to reporters that a happy man was one who could leave an exciting soccer match and go home to a warm and loving family.

In 1966 Pelé needed Rosemarie's support more than he ever had before, for besides being the year of his marriage it was also the year of Pelé's most disappointing and painful World Cup Tournament. The tournament, held in England that year, began on a negative note for Brazil. While the Brazilian fans were confident that they could win the Jules Rimet Cup for the third time to become the first team ever to do so, those with an inside view were not so confident. Pelé was one of these. While he was in excellent shape himself, and free from injuries, some of his teammates were having problems. Also, there was dissension within the delegation that would go to England. There had been a fight over who would lead the delegation, and as a result the training of the team was very disorganized. Because of such problems, the team's morale was very low, and some of the players had decided the World Cup was lost even before the tournament began. Being a very experienced player, and disturbed by the low morale of his team, Pelé wanted to do something, but there was nothing he could do.

The first game in the World Cup Tournament was against Bulgaria, and Pelé had obviously been marked by his opponents. They set upon him immediately, and many of their rough tactics were not called by the officials. As the game progressed, Pelé became more and more angry, and when the referee did call an offense against him by Bulgaria, he determined to make good on the penalty kick awarded him. When an offense is committed outside the penalty area but close enough to the goal to make the penalty kick almost a certain scoring kick, soccer rules provide for an interesting defensive measure. Four or five defending players may line up with locked arms ten yards from the kicker and try to prevent the score. Four sturdy Bulgarians lined up and locked arms in front of the goal, looks of determination on their faces. But Pelé was just as determined. With one of the most incredible kicks in soccer history, Pelé hooked the ball up and around the line of defenders and into the goal! Brazil won the game 2–0, but it was a very costly win. Pelé had been so roughly treated by the Bulgarian players that it was a wonder he had even finished the game. Almost his entire body was bruised and sore, and once again he had received the injury he feared most: a bruise to his left knee.

Pelé sat out the next game against Hungary, nursing his injured knee. By the day of the third game, against Portugal, he had not completely recovered, but he had determined to play anyway. He knew how much his team needed him and how the Brazilian people were counting on him. It was a dark and drizzly day, but the stadium was packed with spectators willing to brave the weather in order to see Pelé play. They greeted him with thunderous applause when he trotted out onto the field and took up his position.

But once again it would be a painful afternoon for Pelé. From the beginning, two Portuguese players seemed intent on putting him out of action, chasing him more than the ball, subjecting him to violent fouls. Pelé tried to play his usual game while at the same time keeping out of their way, but at last they caught up to him, one on either side, and forced him to the ground, crushing him between them.

When the tangle of bodies was cleared, one figure remained on the muddy turf. Pelé did not get up. A hush fell on the crowd as the Brazilian trainer ran out to revive him and his teammates gathered around. English policemen quickly took up positions on the field to keep the spectators in the stands. Slowly, Pelé got up, but there was no cheering from the crowd. He was obviously dazed and hurt. Supported by a man on each side, he slowly hobbled off the field, the rain soaking his already muddied uniform. As the dazed player limped past him, one of the policemen took off his greatcoat and placed it gently around Pelé's shoulders. Wrapped in the huge coat, Pelé looked like a hurt child.

Brazil was eliminated from 1966 World Cup competition; in fact, the team did not even place among the top four. It was a national disgrace, and the Brazilian people, capable of giving so much praise and honor to its winning teams, showed they were just as capable of hating and scorning a losing team. For months afterward, police had to guard the home of the Brazilian coach to keep arsonists away.

As for Pelé, he had "had it." Back home in Brazil, nursing his injured knee, he expressed his frustration at the rough treatment he received in World Cup games. It just was not worth the risk of permanent injury, the risk to his career, to play in the World Cup. He vowed he would never again participate in the premier world soccer competition.

Fortunately, Pelé's knee healed, and by the late summer of 1966 he was ready to accompany the Santos team on a round of exhibition games in various foreign countries, including the United States. On Labor Day, Yankee Stadium in New York City played host to a match between Santos and Internazionale of Milan, Italy. As usual, Pelé was tripped and roughed up, but the crowd, not as usual, did not protest this treatment. New York City has a large Italian population, and the crowd that day was predominantly behind the Internazionale team. Not only was the crowd against him that day, but luck seemed to be against him, too. Two of his goals were disallowed because of off sides (when he made them, there were not two opponents between him and the goal). The one goal he made that was legal was a spectacular one. Taking the ball in front of the goal and seeing an opponent approaching him, he dribbled to his right, drawing the other man with him. Then, suddenly, he reversed direction, raced ahead, and drove the ball into the net. A collective groan rose up from the stands.

Pelé did not mind the lack of crowd support. He was much more interested in the size of the crowd than in who they rooted for. The 41,598 who attended the game was the largest crowd ever to see a soccer game in the United States or Canada. True, they had been attracted by a match between two of the best teams in the world (Internazionale had held the World *Club* Cup the two previous years, and Santos had held it the two years before that) and featuring the greatest player in the world, but whatever had attracted them, they had come. This was important to Pelé. More than for his own Santos team, or for the Brazilian National Team, he was a rooter for soccer itself. He loved the game, no matter who played it, and he was immensely pleased about the increasing acceptance of soccer in the United States.

Early in 1967, he had reason to be pleased again. A game between West Ham United of England and Real Madrid of Spain drew a crowd of 33,351 to the Astrodome in Houston, Texas. Many of the spectators had never seen a soccer game before, but when the match was over the crowd rose to give a standing ovation to both teams. They were applauding not only an outstanding effort by both clubs but also the game of soccer.

That year, 1967, was a contract-signing year for Pelé. It was already two years past the time when, as a twenty-year-old, he had planned to retire. But shortly after his twenty-fifth birthday on October 23, he signed with Santos for three more years at $4,500 per month.

He was still in top physical shape, and he still loved to play soccer, and he saw no reason to retire. Besides, since the age of twenty he had become a living legend in Brazil, and in a way his soccer-playing career was not solely under his control anymore. It belonged, in no small measure, to the people of Brazil, and if there had been any hint that he wanted to retire, public pressure against his leaving the game would have been intense. For the same reason, Pelé did not even seriously consider the attractive offers he received from European clubs. A favorite saying among Brazilians was that the surest cause of a revolution in Brazil would be Pelé's move to another country. Pelé realized there was truth in this saying, and recognized the responsibility it placed upon him. He knew that he would have to retire someday, but as he looked to his future he saw himself playing for Santos for the rest of his soccer-playing days.

In 1967, Pelé scored 57 goals in major-league games; in 1968 he scored 59. This brought his career goal total to 936, and a wave of excitement swept over Brazil. The year 1969 could be the year when he scored his one thousandth goal to become the first player in history ever to do so. Games in which Pelé played were always packed with spectators, but as the 1969 season wore on, the crowds fairly spilled out of the packed bleachers, and there were more than the usual number of fights among fans trying to get into the stadiums. Meanwhile, Pelé's 1969 goal total mounted: 50, 51, 52, 53 . . . 58, 59 . . . the season midpoint passed, and then there were only a few games left. Would he do it in 1969? He did it, and with four goals to spare. His 1969 goal total of 68 brought his career total to 1,004! The one thousandth goal came against the Vasco Da Gama team on November 19, fittingly at the 200,000-seat Maracaña Stadium in Rio de Janeiro, the world's largest sports arena.

Reaching a career total of 1,000 goals is quite an astonishing achievement. Soccer, like hockey, is a relatively low-scoring game, with many match scores only 1–0 or 2–0 or 2–1. To score 1,000 goals in soccer is comparable to averaging 50 points a game in football, or to Henry Aaron's hitting 2,500 home runs.

Once again, Brazil celebrated, and immediately the pressure began for Pelé to reconsider his decision not to play again in World Cup competition. Brazil could win in 1970, and it was Pelé's responsibility to lend his talents to the effort.

At first, Pelé stood firm. He had announced he would not play in future World Cup Tournaments, and he intended to stick to his decision. But the adverse publicity and fan reaction became overwhelming. He was going through a bad phase in his playing, in which he was not making as many goals, not making moves on the field as easily. Ordinarily, the fans would have understood it was just a bad time for him and not taken him to task for it. But Pelé had refused to play in the World Cup Tournament, and the fan reaction to his difficult phase was one of scorn. Their attitude was: "No wonder he doesn't want to play for the Cup, he's no good anymore."

Newspapers carried reports that he was having problems with his eyes, with his knees, that he was not in any condition to play. He was even booed when he played at the huge Maracaña Stadium.

Pelé was very upset. He knew he must play in the World Cup Tournament, and play well, in order to prove himself. And so he agreed to play, although he dreaded the rough treatment he expected to receive. He tried to marshal his own forces, to regain his confidence, to restore his faith in himself.

The Brazilian National Team that went to the 1970 World Cup Tournament in Mexico was a much more "together" group of players than the 1966 team. There were no fights among the team leaders; they traveled together and got along well together, and all were confident that they had a good chance at winning the World Cup. Before going to Mexico they engaged in rigorous physical training, the most organized and well-run training, in Pelé's opinion, of any Brazilian National Team he had been on. By the time they went to Mexico, they could run for ninety minutes easily, and for ninety minutes more if necessary. All this concentration and training helped Pelé with his own problems as well as the team.

Contrary to his expectations, Pelé was treated surprisingly well by his opponents in the 1970 World

Cup Tournament. His announcement four years earlier that he would not play again because the brutality against him had generated considerable worldwide publicity, and this may have been one reason for the better treatment he received in 1970. Another factor was the host country of the 1970 World Cup games. There was no question that the Mexicans favored the Central and Latin American teams, and that Pelé was nearly as popular there as he was in his own country. Also, since Mexico was not too far away from Brazil, there were a large number of Brazilian fans in Mexico City. Any team that tried to trip and maul Pelé would have reason to fear for its safety while in Mexico.

During the qualifying matches the team was full of confidence, and their adversaries could feel it. Pelé scored six times in six games, and with each game he grew more confident and was beset with fewer problems. He continued to contribute and to assist in goals in the last round of competition. In the final game against Italy, he made a brilliant head goal that put Brazil ahead for the first time in their 4–1 victory. But in this tournament, as many other times in Pelé's career, some of his intricate and exceptional moves were actually more memorable than the goals he scored. One such play occurred in an earlier game against Czechoslovakia.

Pelé was dribbling the ball at midfield, and, being far away from the goal, he was not opposed by any of the Czech players. Suddenly, to the surprise of everyone present, he unleashed a fifty-yard lob toward the goal. The Czech goalkeeper, who had been way up at the edge of the penalty box in what he thought was a safe position, tried frantically to get back to cover the goal. The shot narrowly missed, but the goalkeeper, looking at Pelé, knew he had been outwitted.

All in all, it was a very crucial tournament for Pelé. Only he knew what he had gone through personally to win the World Cup. At that time, he determined he would definitely not play in the World Cup in 1974. He would not leave soccer on a bad note. It was just too risky to give an adversary another chance in 1974.

Back in Brazil, all previous celebrations of soccer wins paled in comparison to that celebrating the winning of the 1970 World Cup. Brazil was the first team in the history of World Cup competition to win the Cup three times, and thus it was the first country to retire the famous Jules Rimet Cup. On the night he and his teammates won the game against Italy to retrieve the Cup, crowds thronged the streets of São Paulo chanting "Pe-lé! Pe-lé! Pe-lé!" until dawn. After resting for a time, the team took off for a tour abroad, displaying their prize wherever they went. Pelé was given a parade down the Champs-Élysées in Paris and many other honors wherever he went.

For Pelé, 1970 stands out as the banner year of his life, but not only because Brazil clinched its third World Cup title; the other reason was that his son, Edson Cholby do Nascimento, was born. Pelé had longed for a son and, doubtless, like his father before him, one of the first things he did was to look at the infant's tiny legs and dream that one day he would be a great soccer player.

But Pelé's wish that his son might some day play soccer was not so strong that he intended to pressure the boy into playing. He did not want Edinho, as they called the little boy, to be pressured to be like his father. He did not want anyone to compare his son with him. He wanted Edinho to have a happy childhood. "I will always be his friend," Pelé often says, "and we'll be together and happy whether or not he plays."

Unlike his father before him, Pelé would not have to worry about how to manage with another mouth to feed. Pelé's children would never have to know the poverty he had known as a child. Over the years, Pelé had become very wealthy, and a vast commercial empire was developing under his name.

Its basis had been Pelé's first earnings from his play with Santos, earnings that his father had invested wisely. As Pelé's salary had increased, so had his investments, and in a few years his estate had grown so that he had hired professional advisers to manage it. Rosemarie, too, had offered advice, and had proven a very shrewd businesswoman. But the final decisions on what to do with his money were always Pelé's, and more often than not his decisions were correct.

Take the matter of his coffee business. Brazil and coffee are practically synonymous, and there were already numerous coffee companies in the country when Pelé decided to start his own. But established competition did not seem to worry him. He started his company, and within a few years his Café Pelé was the largest-selling brand in Brazil.

His business ventures became many and varied. He acquired controlling interest in a number of industries, including the rubber industry, bought two radio stations and seventy-five apartment houses. He starred in three movies and wrote two songs that made the top of the best-seller charts in Brazil. Whenever possible, he brought relatives and friends into his various businesses. His younger brother, Zoca, had played soccer for a while, but at the age of twenty he had stopped. His reason indicates the remarkable closeness of the do Nascimento family.

When Pelé had first joined the Santos team, he and the rest of the family had realized that all of the hopes of the family rested on him. He had fulfilled those hopes, and thus the family had rallied to help him. Zoca decided that he could best help his brother by going to school to study law in order to be able to advise him on his various businesses. This sounded like a good idea to Pelé. Because of soccer, he had been unable to go to school as much as he should; Zoca could supply the knowledge he did not have. Thus he put Zoca through law school and then hired him to help manage his affairs. Zoca would continue to go to school to help his brother, taking courses in publicity and advertising. He is Pelé's right-hand man.

Pelé also employed retired teammates. In this way, he built up a network of employees who are completely loyal to him and who protect his interests. Meanwhile, his Santos salary continued to climb, as did the sum he earned in bonuses for exhibition games. When the team played such exhibitions in other countries, the players were always paid in cash, and once Pelé shocked customs officials in Salisbury, Rhodesia. They asked him to open his attaché case for inspection. Pelé complied, revealing $100,000 in bills of various denominations. He was arrested and detained for some time until the customs officials were able to verify that he was indeed the great Pelé and that he had been paid all that money for playing soccer. He was paid $10,000 for each exhibition, and he had played in ten by the time he reached Rhodesia.

No matter how rich he became, Pelé did not become a snob. When the Pepsi-Cola Company signed him to a $200,000-a-year contract to serve as head of its worldwide youth soccer program, he insisted that their program for him involve clinics for children instead of cocktail parties. Nor did he lose sight of his poor beginnings. His favorite place for carrying spending money is in his sock!

For Pelé, money is important not for the power it brings but for the freedom it allows. He is able to do what he wants, and after his marriage to Rosemarie he used it to build the kind of house he wanted. Obviously, he had dreamed about the house for years, and it is understandable that a man who, as a boy, had grown up in ramshackle houses so tiny that he and his younger brother and his grandmother all had to sleep in the same room, would be concerned almost more than anything else with a large and comfortable house in which each member of his family would have a room of his or her own. It is also understandable that a star as sought-after as Pelé, whose life was constantly under public observation, would want a home with complete privacy. Such a house was so important to Pelé that he wanted to be involved in every aspect of its planning and building. From the time the first spadeful of dirt was lifted to the time, three years later, when the house was ready to live in, Pelé spent every spare moment supervising and directing the architects and construction workers. As he did not have all that much spare time, what with his soccer playing, his work for the Pepsi-Cola Company, and his various businesses, it is likely that the house would not have taken so long to build had he not insisted on being so intimately involved in the process. It was such an obsession with him that he is even credited with having designed the door-knobs!

The house was a self-contained world. It was surrounded by a high wall and was fortresslike in its security. No one could get inside who was not allowed in. It included a forty-seat movie theater, adjacent to which was a fully equipped professional darkroom. These were for his wife, who is considered an excellent photographer and moviemaker. For Pelé, there was a huge trophy room where thousands of awards, medals, prizes, and commendations were handsomely displayed, and a private soccer field. All this might appear extravagant, but Pelé didn't think so. Someone in his position must live in a fortress. It was not that he disliked people; he had an intense fear of kidnaping, either of himself or of a member of his family. The theater and darkroom? After all, Rosie should be able to follow her interests, and he certainly needed a room for his trophies and a field on which to practice. His purpose was not to display his wealth. If that had been his purpose, the cars in his four-car garage would all have been luxurious cars. He did have a Mercedes, but the other three were two Volkswagens and an Opel.

One thing is certain: Pelé did not dwell on money for its own sake. He was not even certain how much he was worth. "My father told me that when you're working, don't stop to count your money," he would tell reporters.[2]

In the months after the 1970 World Cup Tournament, Pelé began seriously to think about the time when he would stop "working" as a professional soccer player. He was nearly thirty years old, and while he was still in top physical shape, he realized it was inevitable that soon the years would begin to take their toll. He was too proud to be anything but a star player. He loved soccer, but he knew he could continue on a semiprofessional or nonprofessional basis and enjoy himself just as much. He was not ready to make any firm decisions about when he would leave professional soccer, but in 1971 he did make one announcement: He was retiring from the Brazilian National Team and would play in no more World Cup Tournaments. The reaction in Brazil was one of sadness tinged with some disbelief. After all, in 1966 he had vowed never again to play in World Cup competition, and yet he had changed his mind in 1970. Perhaps he would change his mind again in 1974.

Between 1971 and 1974, Pelé continued to play with Santos both in regular league games and in exhibition games, and to pile up impressive goal totals. In the year he turned 33, 1973, he had 52 goals and countless assists. Then came 1974. In anticipation of the World Cup Tournament in June and July, public pressure on Pelé to play in the tournament began to mount. This time, however, Pelé did not change his mind. Although he continued to play with Santos, he refused to play on the National Team. "I had helped Brazil to win three World Cups," he said later. "I had done my part. I thought it was time the younger guys got a chance."[3]

Pelé lost some fans in Brazil as a result of his refusal to play in the 1974 World Cup, and many blamed him for Brazil's poor performance in the tournament, fourth place. This loss did not particularly trouble Pelé. Like any sports superstar, he was familiar with the fickleness of sports fans. In fact, the coolness of some of the fans made his retirement from professional soccer in Brazil easier.

Pelé played his last professional soccer game for Brazil on September 22, 1974, and all his family and friends were there to see it—everyone except his mother. Celeste do Nascimento could not bring herself to attend even her son's last game. For the past eighteen years, she had not been able to summon the courage to attend a game in which Pelé played, and his last game was no exception. She watched a videotape of the game on television, as was her custom. Pelé officially announced his retirement in October 1974, the month he turned thirty-four. It was difficult for him to leave the team with which he had played for nearly twenty years, and he knew it would take time to get used to a life not scheduled around soccer games. But he looked forward to the freedom he would have, and he felt no guilt. He had served his country well, upheld and increased Brazil's national reputation, and contributed more than any other single player to Brazil's dominance of world soccer. He had played in 1,254 regular league games and scored 1,220 goals—nearly one goal per game. Now he deserved to rest. He and Rosie had enjoyed so little time alone together in the fourteen years since they had met. His children were growing up without him. Edinho was four years old; he needed more than a part-time father. And so, in the fall of 1974, fittingly, after scoring his 1,220th goal on a penalty kick against the Guarini team, Pelé chose to retire from active play, although, he assured reporters, he would continue to do everything he could to promote the game of soccer around the world.

7 Pelé Comes to the United States

Pelé may have thought he had retired from his soccer-playing career, but Clive Toye, general manager of the New York Cosmos, had other ideas. Toye, an Englishman by birth who, as soccer writer for the Birmingham *Mail,* first saw a seventeen-year-old Pelé play in the 1958 World Cup in Stockholm, Sweden, wanted Pelé to come to the United States and play for his team. In fact, he had been trying to sign the Brazilian soccer star since 1971, when the Cosmos team was bought by Warner Communications, Inc., and he was hired as general manager.

Warner Communications is a huge complex of companies that is best known for such movies as *The Exorcist* and such recording stars as Frank Sinatra and the Rolling Stones. Until 1971, it had concentrated on movies, records, and other aspects of the entertainment business, such as *Superman* comics; and the decision to buy a sports team appeared to be a radical departure from its customary activities. But Warner had looked at the popularity of professional spectator sports and seen the millions being made in televised athletic events, and decided that professional sports had become an entertainment industry in its own right.

The corporation would have had little trouble acquiring a team in a variety of sports, and had been offered five basketball, two baseball, and several hockey teams. (Most football teams cost a bit more than Warner wanted to spend. Eighteen million dollars was the going price. Anyway, conglomerates were not allowed to own NFL teams.) But Warner Communications, Inc., had passed up all those offers in favor of a team in the least popular "major" sport of all.

"We feel that soccer is the fastest-growing sport," a Warner spokesman has explained. "It's unquestionably the sport of the future."[1]

So, in 1971, Warner paid $25,000 and got itself a soccer team. But while the company heads believed soccer was the "sport of the future," they realized there were things they could do to hasten the arrival of that future as well as to ensure profits. For one thing, they did not just buy the first soccer team that came available. They deliberately chose a New York team. New York is a major sports area, and because it is also the hub of the country's communications media, its teams receive more television, radio, and newspaper coverage than teams in other cities. By purchasing a New York team, Warner assured itself of more nationwide media coverage of its soccer team than of any other soccer team, although at the time even New York coverage of the sport was limited. What the company needed next was a star who would attract all the potential media coverage available in New York, but for the owners of a soccer team this was easier said than done. Soccer stars were not exactly in plentiful supply; in fact, there was not one soccer player who even came close to the stature of a Joe Namath or a Henry Aaron or a Bobby Orr. That's why Clive Toye, the man Warner hired to be general manager of the Cosmos, decided to go after Pelé.

"Pelé was the one superstar we needed to inspire people to play and see soccer," says Toye. "No other figure could possibly do as much."[2]

Even so, Pelé was not widely known in the United States. Frequently, his name was pronounced *peel,* and even many of those who pronounced his name correctly were unaware of the abilities that had made him so famous. Still, those who played or

British children swarm around Pelé whenever he visits their country, and this visit in March 1973 was no exception. Pelé is the idol of children all over the world, and children are Pelé's favorite fans. *(United Press International Photo)*

Pelé displays some of the medals awards he has received during his e: ing career. He has so many awards trophies, including some of the hig awards Brazil gives, that an entire r in his luxurious house in Santos, Br was built to contain them. *(Ur Press International Photo)*

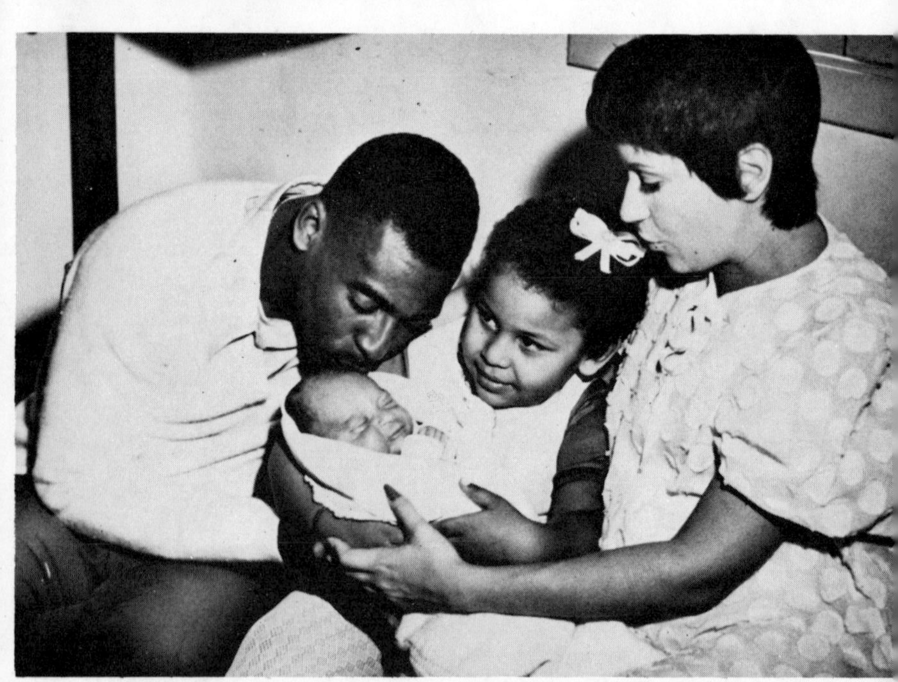

Pelé kisses his newborn son, Edinho, shortly after the baby's birth in 1970, while his wife, Rosemarie, and daughter, Kelly Christina, then age four, look on. Pelé claims that 1970 was the best year of his life—Brazil became the only team in history to win three World Cup championships, and Edinho was born. *(United Press International Photo)*

Soccer is the world's most popular sport, and Pelé is the most famous athlete in the world. In 1971 huge crowds line the Champs-Élysées in Paris to watch him pass by in an open car waving the Jules Rimet Cup, symbol of Brazil's world soccer dominance. In the background is the Arc de Triomphe. *(United Press International Photo)*

Pelé demonstrates some of his ballwork during a visit with President Ford in June 1975. Pelé hopes to help make soccer as popular in the United States as Mr. Ford's favorite game, football. *(Wide World Photos)*

followed soccer in the United States were very aware of him, and many others knew of him, chiefly through news reports of riots at Latin American soccer games in which he played. So Clive Toye began to "court" him.

In the same year that Warner Communications, Inc., bought the Cosmos, Toye traveled to Jamaica, where Pelé was playing with the Santos team. Aware that Pelé was thinking about retiring in a couple of years, Toye asked him to "remember the Cosmos" when making his plans for the future. After that, Toye visited Pelé from time to time in various countries where the Santos team was playing, and reminded him that the Cosmos were still interested.

The "big push," however, came after Pelé actually did retire at the end of the 1974 season. In October 1974 he officially retired from the Santos team, and so firm was his decision that he did not even play in the 1974 World Cup Tournament, much to the consternation of his countrymen. Immediately, Toye began an international "sales campaign" reminiscent of some of Henry Kissinger's assignments. Altogether, he would travel some seventy-five thousand miles, visiting Pelé in Frankfurt, Brussels, Rome, São Paulo, and a variety of other cities. Each time the two met, Toye stressed how important Pelé could be to soccer in the United States if he signed with the Cosmos, how he could be a missionary of soccer to the country—*and* how he would be well paid for his missionary work.

Pelé listened, at first, but refused to commit himself. He had a lot of thinking to do about the offer. He had been playing professional soccer for eighteen years, and he had reached the pinnacle of his career. While his body was still a finely tuned instrument, and while he was in excellent shape, he realized he was old as a soccer player. He had to consider as objectively as he could the possibility that he just might not be able to maintain his previous level of performance. No proud athlete wants to continue playing beyond his effectiveness; he does not want fans and sportswriters to say he doesn't "have it" anymore.

Pelé also had to consider the circumstances of moving his family to the United States. Brazil was his country, his roots were there, his home was there. He knew little of the United States, not even its language. Moving to the United States would mean transplanting his family, taking his children away from their schools and their friends. How would they react? In Brazil, where they were known, his family did not suffer from racial discrimination; but would they receive the same treatment in the United States?

Still, he had to admit there would be advantages in not being so well known in the United States as he was elsewhere. He remembered when, a couple of years back, he and Rosie had walked down Hollywood Boulevard in Los Angeles unrecognized. This could never have happened in Brazil, or in most other parts of the world. Suddenly, he had realized that, and lifting Rosie into the air he had shouted, "I'm free! I'm free!" Privacy. For more years than he cared to remember, it had been denied him. Perhaps in the United States he could enjoy it. Perhaps he would be able to go fishing in peace, to go to a restaurant for steak or lobster without being mobbed.

But what about the people of Brazil? Even though he had helped his country reach the 1974 World Cup Tournament, he had refused to play in the championship on the ground that he had made a definite decision to retire from soccer. Would his Brazilian fans understand if he now went back on his decision? He knew that some, at least, would not. They would be angry and would call him a sellout and a traitor. Pelé had always cared very much about what his fans thought of him; it would hurt him deeply if they turned against him.

He did not like the idea of going back on his word, which he would essentially be doing if he accepted Toye's offer. Pelé was a stubborn man, and a man who was known for forming an idea, or making a decision, and usually sticking to it. Could he change his mind and still live with himself?

Pelé considered these questions, and many more. He considered the money he would be offered; he was certain it would be a multimillion-dollar contract, taking into account both salary and expected income from advertisements, product endorsements, and television and radio appearances.

Meanwhile, Clive Toye persisted, and in March 1975 a major breakthrough occurred when he visited Pelé at the GB Motor Inn near the Brussels, Belgium, airport. Pelé was on a stopover between flights on his way to Morocco, and Toye only had a few minutes to talk with him. Yet Toye was hopeful, for he had received word through Pelé's adviser that the retired soccer star was willing to discuss the possibility of coming out of retirement.

Almost as soon as Toye entered the hotel suite, Pelé confirmed what his adviser had said: "I think it is possible I will play again. I would like to hear your offer."[8] In seconds, Toye told him the basic offer Warner Communications, Inc., was prepared to make.

Pelé listened. Then, without a word, he took a piece of hotel stationery and wrote: "Pelé's last offer." He then wrote a sum and a specific number of years, and signed "Edson=Pelé."

"That was the moment that I first thought we would get him,"[4] Toye recalls. Toye picked up the piece of GB Motor Inn stationery and got back to New York as fast as he could.

It took two more months for the corporation to get Pelé, who changed his mind a few times, and several thousand more miles of travel for Toye, who had to negotiate contract clauses and assure Pelé that the offer was real. But finally, late in May, Pelé and Warner Communications came to an understanding. For Pelé, all the questions he had thought about had, in the end, boiled down to one, and it had nothing to do with his family, or his reputation, or money. It had to do with the game of soccer and his lifelong love of the game. He had received offers to come out of retirement from many countries where soccer was the most popular sport, but he had hardly considered them. These countries, he felt, did not need him. The United States did.

"Maybe I need one more challenge in my lifetime," he has said. "Once in a while it is necessary to have an obstacle to jump over. I would like to introduce my game to this country; it would help make us all brothers."[5]

When it was officially announced that Pelé would sign with the Cosmos, the story made headlines around the world. It was nothing new for people in most other countries to see Pelé's name on the front pages, but for people in the United States it was a "first" to open to the sports section of their favorite newspaper and see a lead story devoted to him. And, of course, when they read about Pelé they read about soccer, and a lead story about soccer was highly unusual. Suddenly, people across the country were talking about soccer with the kind of excitement usually reserved for football.

On June 9, 1975, Pelé left Brazil to join the Cosmos, and the morning after, he was the subject of yet another headline in the major São Paulo newspaper. It was very different from the other headlines that had been appearing in newspapers around the world. It read: BRAZIL'S FIRST DAY WITHOUT PELÉ.

On June 10, 1975, Pelé officially signed his contract with the Cosmos at a packed news conference at the 21 Club in New York. Reporters and photographers from national and foreign newspapers and news services jostled one another to get a better view of him or to ask him a question, and here and there a fist fight broke out. It was all quite unfamiliar to the Cosmos' management and team members who attended the signing. When the team started, as one veteran Cosmo put it, "you could put our press coverage in a . . . closet."[6]

On the platform, Pelé did the best he could to ignore the blinding flashes of photographers' lights, and to answer the rapid-fire questions that came from the reporters. He had to answer most by means of an interpreter, his trainer, Julio Mazzei, who had also joined the Cosmos. But whenever Pelé could, he tried out his English, which he had begun to study after he and Toye had met in Brussels.

"Listen," he said in English, "I have to start in English sometime. I promise for you that after three months when I live here you may come to me and we will speak in English."

Reporting on the event, few newsmen failed to remark on his politeness, his patience. It was behavior they were not used to from superstars. This is not to say that Pelé was not like other superstars in his opinion of his playing prowess. Asked how many goals he expected to get for the Cosmos that season, he replied:

"Well, there are fourteen games left and it will take me ten days to get in top shape, so I would say fourteen or fifteen goals."[7]

Listening to that statement, the Cosmos' management and other players prayed that it would come true.

Almost immediately after his arrival, Pelé was placed on public exhibition. On the evening of the day he arrived, he attended, as a spectator, a game in Philadelphia between the Cosmos and the Philadelphia Atoms. Over twenty thousand fans turned out for the game, double the crowd that usually came, proving that Pelé, even in civilian clothes, had tremendous crowd-drawing appeal. Used to such situations, Pelé seemed unconcerned. He kept a low profile, sitting in a private box, holding hands with Rosie.

Perhaps the large number of spectators worked against the Cosmos in that game, however. It may have made them nervous. Or maybe the presence of their famous new teammate caused them to try too hard to impress him. Whatever the reasons, the Cosmos played dismally that evening, and if it had not been for a tremendous effort on the part of their goalie, Sam Nusam, the score might have been highly embarrassing. The Atoms, who played well as a team throughout the game, managed to score only one goal, and that was in overtime. However, their excellent attempts to score other goals were many. The Cosmos, by contrast, got off very few good goal shots. All night, they seemed to be in the wrong positions, and they could not seem to work together in setting up any sort of effective play. Watching his teammates, Pelé began to realize just how much work he was going to have to do.

Pelé worked out with the Cosmos for the first time in the gymnasium at Long Island's Hofstra University. Rain poured down all day, and Pelé's chauffeur got lost and delivered him there thirty-five minutes late. Normally, players must pay a $25 fine for such an infraction, but it was waived for Pelé. The rest of the Cosmos had been making an attempt at practicing, but everyone was really waiting for the star. Many had dreamed of one day meeting him; none had ever imagined they would some day be playing with him. Pelé was aware of their awe, and while he was flattered, he knew that it was not good. "I've always been a team man and I still am," he told his new teammates. "Please don't expect me to win games alone. We must work together."[8]

The next day, as the team worked out at Downing Stadium, their home stadium on Randalls Island off Manhattan, Pelé, who was on time, called to his teammates by name and praised them for good plays. He was trying to make them feel relaxed around him, to feel that they were good enough to play with him, that he was just a member of the team.

But it was a little hard for the other Cosmos to see Pelé as just another player. While they traveled around by bus, he rode in a chauffeur-driven limousine (soon, Pelé decided to ride in the bus with his teammates). They were under instruction from the team trainers. Pelé had brought his own trainer, Julio Mazzei, who was hired by the Cosmos for team coach Gordon Bradley's staff. The impression, naturally, was that while the rest of the team had one boss, Pelé had another.

Still, under Pelé's unmistakable leadership, the Cosmos began to work as a team with their new player, and in the first Cosmos exhibition game in which Pelé played, the team as a whole turned in a very respectable performance, although it was clear that Pelé had not been with them long.

Downing Stadium, called New York's worst sports arena, was filled almost to capacity with foreign dignitaries, some three hundred newsmen from twenty-two countries (the game was televised in thirteen countries, including the United States and Canada), and thousands of fans. While the audience of over twenty-one thousand would have been swallowed up in Brazil's Maracaña Stadium, it was a good crowd for U.S. soccer nevertheless. Before

Pelé, the crowd at Downing Stadium might have been about nine thousand. At the first glimpse of the man most had come to see, the crowd began to chant "Pe-lé, Pe-lé." His presence almost completely overshadowed that of the opposing Dallas Tornadoes' member, Kyle Rote, Jr., son of the former New York Giants football star, who has been called soccer's first American superstar.

Pelé was still out of shape. A few workouts were not enough to bring him back to his preretirement fitness. Thus he had intended to play only the first half of the game. But the way his team played during the first half did not suit Pelé. He played beautifully, and almost scored a goal, as well as giving many passes to set up possible goals for his teammates. But too often, his passes went into empty spaces that his teammates failed to take advantage of. They seemed to hesitate, looking for him to take the lead when they were actually in a better position to do so. At the end of the half, due in large measure to Kyle Rote, Jr.'s control of the air and goalie Ken Cooper's saves, Dallas led 2–0. So Pelé decided to play in the second half as well.

The Cosmos came out strong in the second half. By then, Pelé's teammates had begun to get used to his moves and passes, and there were many fewer mistakes and mix-ups. Ten minutes into the half,

Pelé, using his right foot to dribble the ball, suddenly stopped and made a low, soft pass to teammate Mordechai Shpigler, from Israel. Shpigler converted the pass for a goal. And about ten minutes later, Pelé himself scored. Near the goal, he leaped into the air. Shpigler lofted a pass to him and Pelé, suspended in midair, twisted and headed it into the net. The spectators were awed—it had looked like a slow-motion playback.

As for Pelé, he leaped high and punched the air with joy. It was his 1,221st goal, but one would have thought it was his first! He had the crowd in the palm of his hand. When he pointed out to his teammates where the ball should go, or when he did not make contact with the ball, leaving it for a teammate, the crowd applauded. Those in the stands who knew the game understood what it took to be able to do that; those who were new to soccer were beginning to understand.

The game ended in a 2–2 tie (there are no tie-breakers in exhibition games). Statisticians soon had their results. In ninety minutes he had touched the ball seventy-six times and had lost it only five times. He had done the "right thing" with the ball fifty times. He had taken six shots at the goal, including two with his head. He was not particularly satisfied with his game, feeling he could have done much better if he had been in better shape, but he was optimistic about future games with his new teammates.

"We need a few more games together," he said, "a chance to get to know each other before we can really start playing. But on today's performance I have no doubt we can become a very good team."[9]

In his second game with the Cosmos, a regulation league game against the Toronto Metros, Pelé's optimism seemed well-founded. They were playing to a capacity crowd of 22,500 at Downing Stadium, which was not large enough to admit all the fans who came to see the game. Although he did not score himself, Pelé, barking instructions and calling out verbal support, led the Cosmos to a 2–0 win. Two days later in Boston, however, they lost, even though Pelé scored.

The Boston Minutemen were really "up" for the game with the Cosmos, and they not only had spirit, they also had their own new star, Portugal's Eusebio, known as the Black Panther of Mozambique. In fact, the game was billed as a rematch between the two stars, who had last played against each other in World Cup competition in 1966 in Liverpool, England. At that time, the Portuguese had eliminated the Brazilian team, with Eusebio getting two goals. For Pelé, who was kicked early in the game, it had been his worst World Cup competition.

The game in Boston was in overtime, after the score had been 1–1 at the end of regulation play. Boston had already made one additional goal, making the score 2–1. With minutes left to play, Pelé sent the ball whizzing past the Boston goalie into the net, and leaped into the air with his customary excitement at scoring. Thinking the goal was good and the game over, fans poured out of the stands and onto the field. They wanted to touch him, to get one of his shoes as a souvenir. In their enthusiasm, they knocked him down, and Pelé, clutching his ankle, gave the injury signal to a nearby referee. The crowd, now turned respectful, moved back to make room for him to be carried off the field on a stretcher. Moments later, the goal he had made was disallowed because of a foul. The game ended with Boston winning, 2–1, the Cosmos protesting the game, and an angry crowd of fans protesting the decision on Pelé's goal and concerned that he had been injured. Although it was initially reported that he was uninjured and had simply used a ploy he had used before to escape from an overenthusiastic crowd of fans, actually he *was* injured, though not badly enough to require hospitalization. He suffered a pulled knee muscle and a sprained ankle, and his shirt, shorts, and right shoe had been ripped.

It seemed that soccer had indeed "arrived" in the United States, including the crowd violence it traditionally attracted, but the arrival of this aspect of the game did not at all please the Cosmos' management. For one thing, they were afraid that such crowd behavior would give soccer a bad reputation in the United States and cause better-class fans to hesitate to attend games. The major concern, however, was the danger to Pelé himself; the Cosmos stood to lose a lot if their star was seriously injured and unable to play with the team. Clive Toye demanded additional security for Pelé wherever he played, and if proper security measures were not taken, the Cosmos would start canceling games. As for Pelé himself, he had been "shaken up and scared," and he was disappointed. After years of traveling in secrecy, of being accompanied by a squadron of bodyguards, of playing on fields separated from the stands by ditches and fences and patrolled by tear gas-armed police, of being unable to walk down a street in civilian clothes without being recognized and mobbed, he had looked to the United States as a place where he could find peace, privacy, and safety. The incident in Boston had hardly lent support to his hopes.

Meanwhile, the press, which continued to be filled with articles about Pelé and the Cosmos, was carrying more news of adverse reaction to his joining the club and to his multimillion-dollar contract. Back in Brazil, after an initial period of mourning over the loss of their star, many of his countrymen had become angry. Pelé had insisted, and continued to insist, that he was not betraying Brazil. In fact, he felt he was doing his country a service, in a way. "For the first time in Brazil's history, we are exporting know-how to you instead of importing it," he had said on the day of the contract signing.

But while some Brazilians were proud that their star had been sought after by the United States, and others decided there was nothing they could do about the situation and went about their daily living, still others deeply resented his move. Wrote one New York *Times* reader, a Brazilian living in the United States, "The Brazilian people are not happy to see Pelé go. As a Brazilian, I will not spend my money to see him play for the New York Cosmos. The people back home feel as I do: disgusted. I have received letters from home and he is no longer our hero." Back in Brazil, an assemblyman in the southern state of Rio Grande proposed that Pelé's title of honorary citizen of the state be revoked "because he had disappointed millions of Brazilians."[10]

"Brazilians are very sentimental and talk, talk, talk," says Pelé, "but I'm going to work for Brazil, I'm going to make propaganda for Brazil."[11]

Meanwhile, Pelé's signing with the Cosmos had also caused some resentment in the United States. U.S.-born soccer professionals had traditionally found it hard to get on the starting teams of their clubs, for the competition from foreign-born players was too rough. In fact, the North American Soccer League finally had made a ruling that each of the established teams must have five American-born players and each of the new teams must have three. But more often than not, the American-born players sat out games on the bench, while the foreign-born players did the actual playing. The American-born players complained that they would never develop their skills if they were not allowed to play. The signing of Pelé by the Cosmos and of Eusebio by the Minutemen naturally caused the American-born players to fear that there would be a large number of foreign-born players imported into the United States and that they would lose their jobs. They were certainly correct in assuming that Pelé's move would cause many more foreign players to want to play in the United States. While before acquiring Pelé the Cosmos had received several calls a week from foreign players who wished to play in the

United States, since Pelé's arrival the number of calls per week had numbered in the hundreds. But though both the Cosmos and the other NASL teams were always looking for good players, they were not eager to pack their teams with foreign players. They realized that in order for soccer to catch on in the United States it would have to have native-born stars as well.

Meanwhile, the Cosmos had to contend with a lot of parents of "future soccer stars." If too many foreign players came to the United States, these parents demanded, who would hire their sons when they were ready to play pro soccer?

Pelé took such criticism in stride, to the best of his ability, at any rate, although it hurt him to be criticized and to feel that his motives were not understood. He hoped that eventually those countrymen who resented his move would come to be proud of him. And he hoped that American-born players, present and future, would come to understand that if he helped soccer increase in popularity in the United States they would benefit from the establishment of many new teams. For the time being, however, he had to concentrate on living up to what was expected of him, what the crowds attending the Cosmos' games were coming to see.

He did so admirably, providing an excellent show

at each game, even when he did not actually score, and occasionally showing bursts of scoring brilliance, such as the two goals he scored in the Cosmos' 9–2 rout of the Washington (D.C.) Diplomats late in June. Wherever he played, he broke attendance records. His first western tour with the team saw throngs of spectators turning out to see him. In terms of play, however, it was not very satisfying. The six-game tour included one stretch of three games in five days, a very tiring schedule. In Los Angeles, the Aztecs beat the Cosmos 5–1 before a capacity crowd of over twelve thousand, and Pelé did not score. Though not very happy with the outcome of the game, he was full of praise for the Aztecs: "The way Los Angeles played tonight," he said after the game, "I think they could have beaten West Germany [the current World Cup champions]. But then I think I may have created more problems for the Cosmos. Every team we play wants to beat the Cosmos more because of me—and they play much better. And I have not had the training I need with the team yet. But we are going to play better together."[12]

In the next game, against Seattle, the Cosmos played better together, but not well enough to win. Seattle won 2–0, and Pelé, in addition to failing to score, received a yellow warning card from an official for the first time.

The referee had called him for pushing an opposing player in an illegal manner. "I was explaining to the referee that I had pushed my man off the ball with my shoulder," said Pelé afterward. "That is all right. I did not use my hands, which is *not* all right. So he took out the yellow card and booked me."

He was asked what the referee had said to him. "He said to be quiet," said Pelé, grinning, "so I went back to play."

It was still another example of Pelé's politeness and even-temperedness. "I believe the referee made a mistake," he said later, "but referees make mistakes all over the world."[13]

Always the gracious visitor, Pelé expressed a great liking for Seattle, particularly for its fishing. On a free afternoon, he happily fished from his third-story hotel balcony, which overlooked the harbor. "Fishing I like very much," grinned the man who caught one small sand shark and lost another, too heavy for his line and who prefers a simple bamboo pole to an expensive fishing rod.

He was also generous with his praise of the Seattle team, and refused to give credence to the views of some observers that the Seattle players had been particularly rough on him and that he had been marked heavily, often violently. Naturally, the Seattle players appreciated the fact that Pelé had not taken advantage of the opportunity to criticize them. Before the Cosmos left for Vancouver, one of the Seattle players lent Pelé a pair of tennis shoes, which might seem a rather strange gesture if one did not understand how much those sneakers would help Pelé.

All the fields on which he played during the western tour were covered with Astroturf, a synthetic grass that more and more athletic fields are using because it requires much less care than real grass. However, it is not used in any other country, and it was an entirely new surface for Pelé. On it, his passes sometimes slid by his teammates, and the ball often bounced too high and was difficult to control. In Seattle, the problem he had with the playing surface was made worse by the intense summer heat. "The ball does not run the same," Pelé explained after the Seattle game. "And today I feel like my feet were on fire. But I noticed that the Seattle team used different shoes, so I will try those shoes when we play in Vancouver. And it will be at night there, so the heat will not be so bad. Here the artificial surface gets very hot, my feet were blistered all around the edges, and I was very tired after the game."[14]

In Vancouver, on a cooler surface and wearing the borrowed tennis shoes, Pelé seemed much more in control of the ball. The Cosmos beat the White-caps in the exhibition game, 2–1, and Pelé set up one of those goals with a perfect pass. "I don't like this surface," he sighed, referring to the Astroturf, "but I must play on it."

The Cosmos returned from their western tour holding second place in the Northern Division of the NASL but scheduled to play against the Boston Minutemen at New York's Downing Stadium. The game was a replay of the game played earlier in the season, in which Pelé's goal had been disallowed and the Cosmos had protested to the NASL commissioner. This upcoming game was an important game for the Cosmos, as Boston had just moved into the Northern Division lead, and if the Cosmos could beat Boston, they would take the lead. Many fans knew this, and despite thunderstorms and traffic tie-ups, more than eighteen thousand turned out.

Tired after their road trip, and with first-stringer Mike Dillon out with an injury, the Cosmos played sluggishly during the first half. Boston scored after only six minutes of play, and by the end of the first forty-five minutes the Cosmos had not scored at all. That called for a few lineup changes by Coach

Bradley, and a pep talk in the locker room. No ties, he warned, this had to be a win.

Bradley sent in Mark Liveric at outside left to replace José Siega. Seventeen minutes into the second half, Liveric crossed the ball from the left side to Julio Correa, who shot the ball under the Boston goalie's plunging body and into the net. Siega, Correa, and Pelé leaped into the air in excitement, and their teammates were equally happy. It was their first league goal in 243 minutes of play (the goals against the Vancouver Whitecaps were not league goals, as the Vancouver game was not a league game), and it was just what they needed. Minutes later, after two blocked shots, fullback Luis de la Fuente completed his third shot from outside the penalty area. And minutes after that, Pelé, who had directed the attack throughout, set up the final goal. The Cosmos had managed to turn the game around by scoring three goals in exactly fourteen minutes! The Minutemen did not score again, and with a record of 6 wins, 8 losses, they fell into second place in the NASL Northern Division behind the Cosmos, whose record was now 7–8. It was just about a month since Pelé had joined the Cosmos; at that time their record had been 3–6.

Each time the Cosmos won a game, sportswriters proclaimed that Pelé and the rest of the team had learned to work together. This game was no exception. But then, each time the Cosmos lost a game, the writers sadly informed their readers that the rest of the Cosmos had not yet learned to work with Pelé. The game against the Portland Timbers on July 16 was reported in the latter manner.

The score, 2–1, was hardly a shutout, although this was primarily because of Cosmos goalie Sam Nusam. Had it not been for some excellent saves on his part, the score could have been much more embarrassing for the Cosmos. The entire team played poorly, and even Pelé, who scored the one Cosmos goal, was not the player the fans had expected to see. The game was played in New York's Downing Stadium, and New York fans, when they are dissatisfied with the way their team is playing, can show that dissatisfaction better than fans anywhere else in the country. This goes for stars, too, no matter how big—as Walt Frazier of the Knicks and Joe Namath of the Jets can attest. Pelé was no exception. While he was not singled out particularly, he was booed and hissed just like the other Cosmos.

In the face of all this, even the usually optimistic Pelé was glum. "We played the worst game since I've been here," he said in the locker room afterward. "I hope it won't happen again."[15]

It did. In their next game, against the Toronto

Metros, the Cosmos lost again, 3–0. Far worse than the loss itself, however, was that Pelé was injured in the game. Pulled from behind early in the second half, he injured his left thigh. And though he finished the game and was not taken to the hospital, it was announced that he would not play in the exhibition game scheduled in St. Louis with the Stars two days later.

Reaction from the St. Louis Stars' management revealed just how important Pelé was. They did not want to hold the game if Pelé did not play, and that was that.

The Cosmos were having a run of extremely bad luck, and Pelé's injury was practically the least of it —in terms of the game itself, anyway. Regarding money, the postponement of the exhibition game in St. Louis had cost the Cosmos dearly. Because they had Pelé, they were the only team in the league that received a percentage of the gate receipts at away games. In terms of the league standings, they were now in third place in their division, behind Toronto and Boston. Also, their captain, Barry Mahy, was out for the season with a broken left ankle, and forward Americo Paredes had pulled a hamstring muscle in Toronto. The team had won only seven of seventeen games. Five players, including three starters, were put on waivers, or taken off active duty and offered to other teams. While Clive Toye and others in the Cosmos' management denied it, clearly the team was in a slump.

Meanwhile, Pelé drilled to get his left leg back into shape. A league game against the San Jose Earthquakes was coming up, and though he had decided not to play in the St. Louis exhibition game, a league game was a different matter. He was too much of a veteran to miss a league game if he could possibly help it, just as he had been too much of a veteran to leave the Toronto game after he was hurt. Instead, he had played hurt, hobbling at times, refusing to give the signal that he wanted to go out. It proved once again what a great player he was.

Working out so that he could see action against the Earthquakes, Pelé must have been having some private second thoughts about his decision to come to the United States to play with the Cosmos. He was being forced to play on a strange kind of turf, under conditions that were different from those under which he had played for eighteen years. It had taken him much longer than he had expected to get back into shape after coming out of retirement, and he worried about this and future injuries. He knew his body no longer had the same resiliency. While he tried not to think about it, the fear of playing beyond his prime, of making embarrassing mistakes, was sometimes present. Still, he had so far been successful in his stated reason for leaving retirement and coming to the United States, and he was not one to dwell on his problems or to give up very easily.

On July 23, 1975, the Cosmos began to pull out of their slump, beating the San Jose Earthquakes, 2–1 at Downing Stadium before a crowd of forgiving fans. The Earthquakes, who did not play any better than the Cosmos in the first half, took the lead eighteen minutes into the second half and held it until the game was practically over. Then, with a little more than four minutes left to play, Pelé read a play that was to go to the Earthquakes' goalie, intercepted the pass, and put it into the net. But he did not even accept his teammates' congratulations. The game was only tied, he reminded them, it was not won. And Pelé was determined to win this game, for his own sake as well as that of his team. In overtime, neither team scored, and so the final attempt to decide a game was employed. Each team was given five penalty kicks. The Cosmos made all theirs; Cosmos' goalie Kurt Kuykendall saved one of the Earthquakes' penalty kicks.

Perhaps one reason why Pelé displayed an uncharacteristic grimness during the San Jose game was that his left thigh was still paining him. Observers noted that he seemed hurt. Yet he still played in the team's next game in Dallas, and he was glad he had. Before the start of the game, he got a standing ovation from the twenty-six thousand fans as he circled the stadium, flashing the victory sign. "I cried when I ran the lap around the field," he said later. "It was a very emotional experience."[16]

Seventy minutes into the Dallas game, however, he was toppled, and fell on his left leg. He had to leave the game, and he was advised that unless he rested completely for a few days, he would only further aggravate his injury. This meant he would miss at least the next two games. With only four games left in the regular season—four "must wins" if the Cosmos were to have a chance at the play-offs—it was quite a blow to the team.

Pelé did return to finish off the regular season, but at the end the Cosmos' record was not good enough for the play-offs. In fact, any remaining hopes for a play-off spot were dashed in the first week of August when the Cosmos, playing without the injured Pelé, lost to the Hartford Bicentennials, 3–1. Losing later to the Boston Minutemen, 5–0, was like rubbing salt into the wound. Failing to make the play-offs was unfortunate not only for the Cosmos but for the NASL as well, for a play-off series in which Pelé was involved would have drawn much larger crowds than a series without him. Still, attendance at play-off games showed a notable increase over that of previous years. Pelé was the big crowd attraction, but more fans were beginning to attend games out of interest in soccer itself.

It is too early to tell if soccer will ever equal the other major professional sports in popularity, let alone surpass them. Yet there is no question that interest in soccer is rising. By 1975 the NASL had twenty teams, and with six hundred colleges already playing some form of soccer in the United States, not to mention the high school, youth, and amateur clubs, it is likely that the NASL will continue to expand and will come to rely less and less on foreign players. Newspaper and magazine coverage, and most importantly television coverage, is increasing. Most of this expanded coverage is due to Pelé, for a superstar, no matter in what country or in what sport, attracts the media. Articles on Pelé have led to articles on other soccer players. New York newspapers, for example, were full of the name of Pelé in the summer of 1975, but here and there they carried articles on other Cosmos, present and past. Elsewhere around the country, local newspapers began to take a greater interest in the players on the teams in their areas. Television coverage of soccer during the first

Pelé season was greater than it had ever been before, and attendance at Cosmos games, whether at home or on the road, just about doubled. But many of those who watched the games on television or attended the games to see Pelé, became interested in soccer at the same time and began to watch and attend games even when hc was not playing. All this, of course, is what Pelé's coming to the United States was really all about.

When he had first arrived, there had been some speculation about what nickname he would be given in the United States. He was "Black Pearl" in Brazil, "The King" in Italy. What would the "gringos" call him? Surprisingly, he has been given no nickname; he is simply called Pelé. What has happened is that his nickname has begun to be adopted as a synonym for "the greatest." Cooking expert Julia Child has been called "the Pelé of the kitchen." Singer Beverly Sills has been described as "the Pelé of grand opera." In the United States, there is no higher honor than this use of a person's name.

As for Pelé himself, he has decided that the advantages of coming out of retirement and signing with a U.S. team outweigh the disadvantages. Very interested in the statistics on game attendance and press coverage of soccer since his arrival, he is secure in the knowledge that he is indeed helping to put soccer on the United States map. In terms of his own performance, he is not particularly satisfied. He has been plagued by injuries. He had hoped to score fourteen or fifteen goals in his first season with the Cosmos; he'd scored only seven, and only five in league games. But he realized it would take more than part of a season to get back into shape after an eight-month retirement, and that it would take time for him and the other Cosmos to learn to work together as a team.

Meanwhile, he would be making a lot of money. The Cosmos' off-season exhibition games would draw huge crowds of people eager to see Pelé, and he would be paid for each one. At the same time, he would be making money from advertisements, product endorsements, and commercials for everything from shoes to sports equipment to men's cologne. Late in the summer of 1975, Fabergé, manufacturer of the Brut men's line, signed Pelé to a worldwide advertising campaign in which he would make TV commercials in English, Portuguese, and Spanish. Joe Namath, a sports adviser to the company, helped to select him.

As to his private life, Pelé and his family were adjusting to their new home in New York, where they would spend about ten months of the year, going back to their home in Brazil for about two months each year. The children were enrolled in the United Nations School, where they made new friendships with children of many different nationalities. Reading newspapers and watching television, Pelé realized that there were greater racial animosities in the United States than in Brazil. But he did not personally find evidence of them. "Here," he said in an interview after coming to the United States, "everybody seems to work together. The restaurants are full of people of all colors; in the police cars I see a white sitting beside a black. Maybe in other parts of the nation it is different."

Perhaps most important for Pelé personally was the comparative privacy he had come to enjoy in the United States. While he had been besieged for countless interviews by representatives of the media, and while he had been mobbed once in Boston, he no longer had to travel with a phalanx of bodyguards or move about in secret. He was doing the thing he loved most of all—playing soccer—in an environment that held what he valued for himself most of all: more privacy than he had known in years. As he has said, ". . . the United States has lots of famous people in movies and sports. Here I will just be one of many stars."[17]

Pelé is hardly just "one of many stars." He may well be the greatest star in professional sports history, and people in the United States are now part of what someone has called "the luckiest generation in history because it has seen Pelé play." It is doubtful that there will be another Pelé for many generations to come.

Glossary of Selected Soccer Terms

BLOCKING Also called obstructing, a method of slowing the forward progress of an opponent by moving slowly in front of him and forcing him to change direction.

CENTER KICK A kick made from near the sidelines toward the center of the field for the purpose of setting up a score.

CHARGING A method used to unbalance an opponent by jostling him with the shoulder. One foot must be kept on the ground.

CHIP A short, sharp kick that lifts the ball over the opponent's head.

CLEARING KICK A kick that sends the ball away from the goal and toward the other end of the field.

CORNER KICK A kick awarded to the offensive team when a member of the defensive team is last to touch the ball before it goes over the goal line but does not score. It is a penalty kick, but as it is made from the corner of the field near the goal, a score is possible only with a hard curve.

CROSS A kick from one side of the field to the other.

DIVING A method employed by the goalkeeper to stop the ball by throwing himself upon it.

DRIBBLING Controlling and moving the ball with the feet while running down the field.

FLICK PASS A short kick of the ball to one side to a teammate, usually made while dribbling.

FOUL Illegal use of the hands or the body, usually in the process of charging or blocking.

GOAL KICK A kick awarded the defensive team after a member of the offensive team is last to touch the ball before it goes over the goal line but does not score. It enables the defense to get the ball out of danger and toward the other end of the field.

HEADING Using the head, specifically the center part of the forehead, to hit the ball in midair.

INTERCEPTION Cutting off an offensive team's pass; this is a legal action.

MARK To watch and follow an opponent to prevent him from getting the ball.

OBSTRUCTING The same as blocking.

OFF SIDE An illegal situation in which there are no defenders except the goalkeeper between an attacker and the goal.

PASSING Kicking the ball from one teammate to another to move it downfield or set up a goal.

PENALTY KICK A free kick toward the goal. If the foul for which the kick is awarded occurred within the penalty area, or the zone in front of the goal, only the goalkeeper can defend the goal against it. If the foul occurred outside the penalty area, four or five defending players can line up with locked arms in front of the goal ten yards from the kicker.

SAVE An action of the goalkeeper to prevent a score.

TACKLING A method to get the ball away from an opponent through clever use of the feet, and without tripping the other man.

THROUGH-PASS A pass straight forward from an attacker to his teammate.

TRAPPING Getting control of the ball through use of the head, body, legs, or feet to stop the ball when it is approaching either in the air or on the ground.

World Cup Winners

1930 in Uruguay
Champions: Uruguay
Second Pl.: Argentina
Third Pl.: United States
Fourth Pl.: Yugoslavia

1934 in Italy
Champions: Italy
Second Pl.: Czechoslovakia
Third Pl.: Germany
Fourth Pl.: Austria

1938 in France
Champions: Italy
Second Pl.: Hungary
Third Pl.: Brazil
Fourth Pl.: Sweden

1942
No World Cup competition due to World War II

1946
No World Cup competition due to World War II

1950 in Brazil
Champions: Uruguay
Second Pl.: Brazil
Third Pl.: Sweden
Fourth Pl.: Spain

1954 in Switzerland

Champions: West Germany
Second Pl.: Hungary
Third Pl.: Austria
Fourth Pl.: Uruguay

1958 in Sweden

Champions: Brazil
Second Pl.: Sweden
Third Pl.: France
Fourth Pl.: West Germany

1962 in Chile

Champions: Brazil
Second Pl.: Czechoslovakia
Third Pl.: Chile
Fourth Pl.: Yugoslavia

1966 in England

Champions: England
Second Pl.: West Germany
Third Pl.: Chile
Fourth Pl.: Soviet Union

1970 in Mexico

Champions: Brazil
Second Pl.: Italy
Third Pl.: West Germany
Fourth Pl.: Uruguay

1974 in West Germany

Champions: West Germany
Second Pl.: Netherlands
Third Pl.: Poland
Fourth Pl.: Brazil

Pelé's Goals, by Year

1956	2
1957	66
1958	87
1959	127
1960	78
1961	110
1962	71
1963	76
1964	60
1965	101
1966	42
1967	57
1968	59
1969	68
1970	59
1971	34

1972	50
1973	52
1974	21
1975 (5 league games)	5
Total	1,225

Number of games in which Pelé scored 3 goals	90
Number of games in which Pelé scored 4 goals	30
Number of games in which Pelé scored 5 goals	6
Number of games in which Pelé scored 8 goals	1

Number of exhibition games Pelé played in the summer of 1975	5
Number of goals Pelé scored in exhibition in the summer of 1975	2

Pelé's Goals, by Team

Santos (and Santos-Vasco Da Gama)	1,096
Brazilian National Team	95
Military Team	14
Other All-Star Teams	15
New York Cosmos (League Games)	5
Total	1,225

Notes

3 EARLY YEARS

1. Benedito Ruy Barbosa, *Eu Sou Pelé* (São Paulo, Brazil: Editôra Paulo de Azevedo Ltda., 1961), p. 11.
2. Ibid., pp. 19–20.
3. Thomas Mazzoni, *Pelé and the Others,* Rio de Janeiro, Brazil: Editôra do Autor, 1963, p. 12.
4. Ibid., p. 62.
5. Ibid., pp. 64–65.

4 BREAKING INTO THE GAME

1. Ibid., p. 69.
2. Ted Smits, *The Game of Soccer* (Englewood Cliffs, N.J.: Prentice-Hall, Inc., 1968), p. 83.
3. Barbosa, op. cit., pp. 73–74.
4. Ibid., p. 78.
5. Ibid., p. 88.
6. Ibid.
7. Ibid., p. 101.
8. Ibid., p. 5.
9. Ibid., p. 113.
10. Mazzoni, op. cit., p. 45.
11. Barbosa, op. cit., p. 131.
12. Ibid., p. 136.
13. Ibid., p. 142.

5 FROM "IDOL KID" TO BIG CROCODILE

1. Ibid., p. 151.
2. Ibid., p. 161.
3. New York *Times* (June 10, 1975).
4. Peter Bodo and Dave Hirshey, "The Pelé Phenomenon" (New York *Sunday News,* July 27, 1975), p. 24.
5. Ibid.

6 PELÉ SETTLES DOWN

1. Barbosa, op. cit., p. 185.
2. New York *Times* (June 8, 1975).
3. Mark Goodman, "The Pearless Pelé Comes to Gotham to Put U. S. Soccer on the Map," *People* magazine (August 4, 1975), pp. 54–57.

7 PELÉ COMES TO THE UNITED STATES

1. New York *Times* (July 27, 1975).
2. Ibid.
3. New York *Times* (June 5, 1975).
4. Ibid.
5. Bodo and Hirshey, op. cit., p. 18.
6. New York *Times* (June 11, 1975).
7. Ibid.
8. Jerry Kirshenbaum, "Curtain Call for a Legend," *Sports Illustrated* (June 23, 1975), p. 20.
9. New York *Times* (June 16, 1975).
10. New York *Times* (June 4, 1975).
11. New York *Times* (June 5, 1975).
12. Tex Maule, "Yes, It'll Play in Peoria," *Sports Illustrated* (July 21, 1975), p. 49.
13. Ibid., pp. 52, 54.
14. Ibid., p. 52.
15. New York *Times* (July 17, 1975).
16. New York *Times* (July 30, 1975).
17. Kirshenbaum, op. cit., p. 21.

Selected Bibliography

"A $4.5 Million Gamble," *Time,* June 30, 1975, pp. 56–57.

Barbosa, Benedito Ruy. *Eu Sou Pelé.* São Paulo, Brazil: Editôra Paulo de Azevedo Ltda., 1961.

Bayer, Bob. "Pelé," *The Brasilians,* May–June 1975, p. 25.

Bodo, Peter, and Hirshey, Dave. "The Pelé Phenomenon," New York *Sunday News,* July 27, 1975, pp. 17–24.

Bonventre, Peter. "A Boot for Pro Soccer," *Newsweek,* June 30, 1975, p. 43.

"Can Pelé Bring the Big Payday to U.S. Soccer?," *Ebony,* Sept. 1975, pp. 136–38ff.

Do Nascimento, Edson Arantes. *Jogando lom Pelé.* Rio de Janeiro, Brazil: José Olympio Editora, S.A., 1974.

"For the Record," *Sports Illustrated,* June–Aug. 1975.

Goodman, Mark. "The Peerless Pelé Comes to Gotham to Put U.S. Soccer on the Map." *People* magazine, August 4, 1975, pp. 54–57.

Indianapolis *Recorder,* June–Aug. 1975.

Indianapolis *Star,* June–Aug. 1975.

Jornal Do Brasil, Special Supplement. Rio de Janeiro: Oct. 4, 1974, pp. 1–15.

Kirshenbaum, Jerry. "Curtain Call for a Legend," *Sports Illustrated,* June 23, 1975, pp. 18–21.

Maule, Tex. "Yes, It'll Play in Peoria," *Sports Illustrated,* July 21, 1975, pp. 49–54.

Mazzoni, Thomas. *Pelé and the Others.* Rio de Janeiro, Brazil: Editôra do Autor, 1963.

Moynihan, John. *Soccer.* New York: Thomas Y. Crowell Company, 1974.

New York *Post,* July 2, 1975, p. 60.

New York *Times,* June–Aug. 1975.

"People Are Talking About . . . ," *Vogue,* Aug. 1975, p. 120.

Smits, Ted. *The Game of Soccer.* Englewood Cliffs, N.J.: Prentice-Hall, Inc., 1968.

JAMES S. HASKINS has taught in elementary and junior high schools, the New School for Social Research, the New York State University College at New Paltz, Staten Island Community College, and Indiana University—Purdue University at Indianapolis. He is also an educational consultant, a book reviewer, and the author of a number of books for adults and young people. His first book was the highly praised *Diary of a Harlem Schoolteacher. Witchcraft, Mysticism and Magic in the Black World* is the result of his long interest in the strength of African religious and spiritual customs and the central role they have played historically in the survival of black people. He has also written *Resistance: Profiles in Nonviolence, Profiles in Black Power,* and *Jokes from Black Folks* for Doubleday & Company, as well as *Doctor J: A Biography of Julius Erving,* published in 1975.